NEW ADMIRALTY

TIDAL CURVES

Since this edition of Pass Your Yachtmaster's was prepared, the Hydrographer has changed the presentation of tidal curves in Volume I of the Admiralty Tide Tables. However the principles are exactly the same. The purpose of the new presentation (which the nautical almanacs have to a large extent followed) is merely to enable you to read off times or heights graphically, instead of calculating them arithmetically. The new method does the sums for you, in other words. You should find it simpler and quicker. But it does mean that although the general explanation of tides on pages 24–28 of P.Y.Y. is still correct – and particularly as far as the Rule of Twelfths is concerned – the curves you will now find in the Tide Tables look rather different.

Turning to the pages dealing with Dover, the times and heights of high and low water for this 'standard port' are laid out as before for each day of the year (times in GMT, heights now only in metres). Alongside, the two tidal curves – a solid line and a dashed line for springs and neaps respectively – are superimposed one on the other. Their humped shape shows why the Rule of Twelfths works, and at Dover, though not always elsewhere (see for example Lowestoft or Portsmouth) the tide accelerates and slackens in much the same way whether it is springs or neaps.

The new feature is on the left hand side of the diagram. This refers to the height of the tide, marked along top and bottom in metres above chart datum. Its purpose is to relate the 'shape' of the tide's rise and fall to the actual levels of low and high water on a particular day. The mean levels at high water springs (MHWS), low water springs, high water neaps and so on, are already marked.

To use the curves, you extract the relevant times and heights of HW and LW on the day you need from the accompanying table and apply them to the diagram. The time of HW and the hourly intervals before and after it can be written in the boxes beneath the curves (remembering to convert from GMT to BST if necessary); the heights of HW (x1) and LW (x2) must then be marked off along top and bottom respectively, and joined with a sloping tide line (x). The diagram now contains all the information needed for one of the two basic calculations.

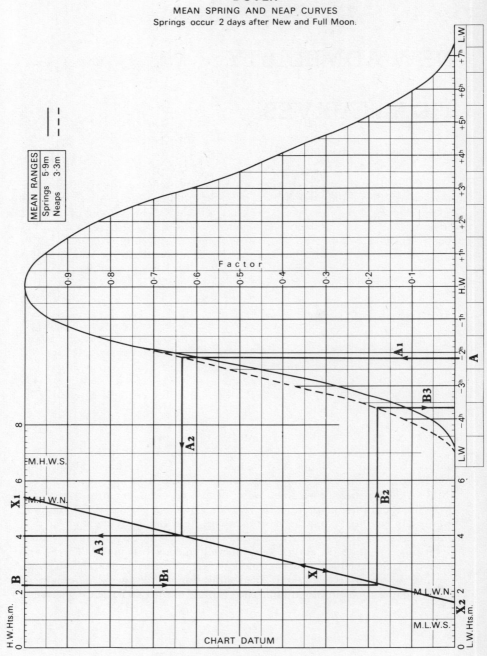

To find the height of tide (at a standard port) at a given time between high and low water:

(i) calculate how many hours before or after HW your given time is, and mark it along the base of the curves (A);

(ii) from this starting point, draw a line vertically to meet the appropriate curve (springs or neaps) (A1);

(iii) proceed horizontally to meet the sloping tide line showing the relevant range on the required day (A2);

(iv) proceed vertically, up or down, to read off the height at your given time (A3).

To find the time at which the tide will reach a given height (at a standard port):

(i) starting from the required height on the horizontal height scale (B), draw a line vertically to meet the sloping tide line (B1);

(ii) proceed horizontally to the appropriate curve (springs or neaps, rising or falling) (B2);

(iii) proceed vertically down to read off the time before or after HW on the horizontal time scale (B3).

There will naturally be many occasions when a calculation of the range (HW–LW) shows that this is neither a spring nor a neap tide, but something in between. If the two curves for that port are significantly different, the Hydrographer suggests interpolating between them by eye, according to the relationship between the actual range and the ranges shown for springs and neaps. Reed's almanac uses an arithmetic method for this calculation, which also serves to interpolate between time and height differences at secondary ports. An explanation of the Admiralty's method of dealing with secondary ports, together with examples of the basic time and height calculations described above, will be found at the beginning of the Tide Tables.

For those sailing in the Isle of Wight area, or calculating its tides, there is one final complication. Between Swanage and Selsey, the shape of the tides is greatly distorted – so much so that some ports have a double high tide. Fortunately, low tide remains a single, clearly identified event, so for the standard port of Southampton, the Admiralty's tidal curve is centred on low water, not high water. But the methods of calculation remain the same.

In addition, the Hydrographer provides individual curves for many of these popular yachting centres, even though they are only secondary ports, and these curves too are centred on low water. For several of them, where the difference between the spring and the neap shape is large, a third line is added to make interpolation more accurate.

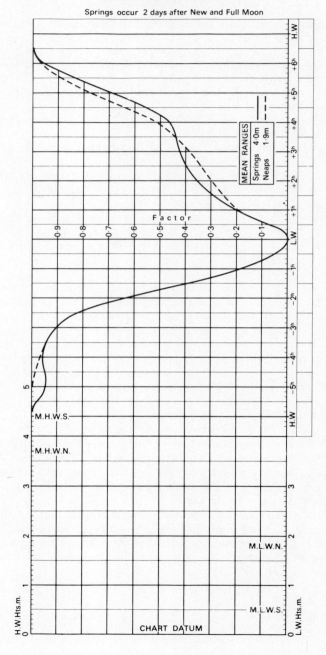

Pass Your Yachtmaster's

Pass Your Yachtmaster's

David Fairhall and Mike Peyton

Copyright © David Fairhall and Michael Peyton 1982

All rights reserved. No part of this publication may be reproduced or transmitted, in any form or by any means, without permission.

First published in Great Britain 1982 by
NAUTICAL BOOKS
An imprint of Conway Maritime Press Ltd
24 Bride Lane, Fleet Street,
London EC4Y 8DR

Reprinted (with corrections) 1983
Reprinted 1986

Composition in Sabon by Filmtype Services
Limited, Scarborough, North Yorkshire

Printed by the Bath Press, Bath

British Library Cataloguing in Publication Data
Fairhall, David
   Pass your yachtmaster's
   1. Yachts and yachting – Great Britain
   2. Royal Yachting Association
   I. Title
   797.1'24'076   GV814

   ISBN 0 85177 440 7

CONTENTS

Foreword	vii
Introduction	ix
The syllabus	xi
Signals	1
Navigation	9
Meteorology	39
Safety and seagoing practice	57

This book is dedicated with affection to the memory of Lieut. Commander 'Freddie' Wells Gayford, who ran the Yachtmaster courses at the Maldon Little Ship Club – where the book first got under way.

FOREWORD

Every year thousands of sailors take courses associated with the Yacht-master Offshore Certificate of the Royal Yachting Association (in cooperation with the Department of Trade). This book is concerned with the shorebased Yachtmaster Offshore course, which is combined with a Coastal Skipper course. For these it is in part a 'crammer', which means a students' guide to approaching, revising for and then passing the assessment examinations.

The Yachtmaster Offshore course is only one element of a comprehensive RYA training scheme, whose aim is 'to encourage high standards of seamanship and navigation among yachtsmen'. The chairman of the joint RYA/DoT qualification panel has added two further objectives: to encourage safety on board cruising yachts, and to ensure that 'by a responsible attitude to standards of competence, we may continue to enjoy freedom to go to sea'.

The RYA prefers not to talk about its shorebased courses as an examination process. It emphasizes that students who reach the required theoretical standard are merely awarded certificates for 'satisfactory completion of a course of instruction'. Whereas for the Coastal Skipper qualification, this may be combined with a practical course and an oral examination, plus the necessary seatime, to acquire the final 'certificate of competence', the new rules introduced in 1983 closed this route for the Yachtmaster Offshore, who must in future seek his certificate of competence through a direct practical examination at sea.

This sensible change does not, however, make the shorebased course any less appropriate as an academic preparation for the would-be Yachtmaster – which is what it always was. Its aim is 'to teach navigation, meteorology and signals to the standard required for the navigation of a yacht on coastal and offshore passages not requiring astro-navigation'. It also remains true that whatever the exercises and assessment papers are called, they strike most students as exams of the old-fashioned kind they may not have encountered since leaving school. Some have to be tackled under invigilation, with a time limit which requires careful pacing and detailed knowledge that most people will want to 'swot up' the night before.

These tests are the nearest thing that exists in Britain to a master's ticket for amateur sailors. Master's tickets are evidence of theoretical knowledge by Merchant Navy officers, whatever their actual appointment. It is comparable for a yachtmaster, who may or may not be skippering a sailing yacht (there are alternative tests for motor boat work). Indeed the term 'yachtmaster' came from previous government tests for the handling of small powered vessels, enabling yachtsmen to take charge of them in a national emergency. In 1973 this scheme was dropped in favour of training for today's sailors on sailing or auxiliary yachts, or motor cruisers.

So the RYA training scheme for seagoing yachts is now at five levels: Competent Crew, Day Skipper/Watch Leader, Coastal Skipper, *Yachtmaster Offshore* and Yachtmaster Ocean. The coastal skipper is expected to have 'the knowledge to skipper a cruising yacht on coastal cruises but does not necessarily have the experience needed to undertake longer passages'. The yachtmaster offshore 'is an experienced yachtsman, competent to skipper a cruising yacht on any passage which can be completed without the use of astro-navigation'. The yachtmaster ocean 'is an experienced yachtsman, competent to skipper a yacht on passages of any length, in all parts of the world'.

These courses are intended for sailing yachtsmen, but the Coastal Skipper, Yachtmaster Offshore and Yachtmaster Ocean certificates may be awarded to motor yachtsmen, who will not be asked to demonstrate the ability to sail, but will be expected to have a sound knowledge of marine engine installations.

The Yachtmaster's certificate of competence is awarded after a practical examination at sea, lasting perhaps eight to twelve hours. For this the candidate must provide a seaworthy cruising or offshore racing yacht normally not less than 24 ft LOA. He must also produce a personal log, demonstrating that he has acquired the necessary seatime and experience. A Yachtmaster Offshore must have logged at least 2500 miles in tidal waters, living on board a cruising yacht for a minimum of 50 days. He must have made at least five passages of more than 60 miles, acting as skipper for two of them, and two of the passages must have been overnight. The Yachtmaster Ocean qualification is open only to Yachtmasters Offshore, after completing a shorebased course in astro-navigation and worldwide meteorology, plus a passage of at least 600 miles.

A summary of the combined Coastal Skipper and Yachtmaster Offshore Shorebased Course as published by the RYA will be found on page xi. Absorb these subjects as set out in the book and you are more than sailing on your way to Pass Your Yachtmaster's.

INTRODUCTION

If the Yachtmaster qualifications were easily obtained they would not be worth having. But thousands have already completed the shorebased course, and we think we have found ways of making it easier for others. We have done this by looking for the logic as well as the facts, by eliminating unnecessary information, by presenting the essentials in the form the RYA's shorebased syllabus requires, and by advising on examination tactics. At the same time, we have tried always to remember that the acid test of all this theory is whether in practice it makes you a better sailor.

The idea for the book really goes back to the moment when the authors were themselves confronted with the long list of recommended books for the Yachtmaster Offshore course, only short sections of which were sometimes relevant. If only, we thought, there was a single textbook covering the whole syllabus.

Pass Your Yachtmaster's is an attempt to provide it. No textbook is a substitute for the extensive background reading instructors may recommend, let alone for the instruction itself. But our book does organize all the elements of the shorebased Yachtmaster Offshore and Coastal Skipper syllabus between two covers (plus a note on ropes and ropework, so that apart from a general knowledge of simple nautical terms, which we have assumed, it also covers the otherwise more limited Competent Crew/Day Skipper/Watch Leader syllabus). It is a skeleton waiting to be fleshed out by teaching, by reading, and by practical experience – because ultimately there is no substitute for sea time.

For some readers, much of the material will already be familiar, but no point of principle has been taken for granted, however simple. In each of the main sections – signals, navigation, meteorology and seagoing practice – we have tried to help students in four distinct ways:

(i) by providing all the basic facts, theories, terminology and definitions in the way the syllabus requires

(ii) by organizing this information in a digestible form that makes learning and revision easier – so you can slip the book into your pocket and skim through the subject headings of an assessment paper whenever you have a spare moment, in the lunch hour, on the train home, or just before you go into the examination

(iii) by advising on examination tactics – so that hopefully you *do* pass your Yachtmaster's

(iv) by setting all this theory in a practical, seagoing perspective where some of it still matters and some of it can safely have been left in the classroom – because we hope the book will also be useful to people who never actually take the Yachtmaster examinations, but want to know what the RYA qualification is all about

The shorebased part of the Yachtmaster Offshore course involves completing a number of exercises or assessment papers covering charts and navigational publications, dead reckoning and estimated position, the magnetic compass, position fixing, tides, tidal streams, pilotage and visual aids, a general group of subjects, meteorology, the International Regulations for Preventing Collisions at Sea, and passage making and chartwork.

Some of these have to be done under examination conditions, but the remainder may, at the instructor's discretion, be set as private study and in some cases recourse to reference books is encouraged. There are also tests on Morse Code and the International Code of Signals.

We have covered all these in a logical sequence, though not necessarily in precisely the same order as you will tackle them in your own course. The major changes announced by the RYA in 1983 have been incorporated, but at the time of writing some of the revised instructional material had yet to be published and students may find some detailed changes in, for example, the course notes referred to here. After that it is a matter of accumulating the necessary seatime as you put theory into practice, before taking the final examination for your Yachtmaster Certificate of Competence. We wish you luck.

D.F.
M.P.
Maldon, Essex
July 1983

THE SYLLABUS

The Royal Yachting Association lists the subjects and their subdivisions for the shorebased course as follows:

Subject	*Subdivisions*
1 Definition of position, course and speed	1 Latitude and longitude 2 Knowledge of standard navigational terms 3 True bearings and courses 4 The knot
2 Navigational drawing instruments	1 Parallel rulers 2 Dividers and compasses 3 Proprietary plotting instruments
3 Navigational charts and publications	1 Suppliers – Admiralty, Stanford, etc 2 Information shown on Admiralty charts 3 Chart symbols – Chart 5011 4 Standard chartwork 5 Projections – Mercator and gnomonic 6 Navigational publications in common use 7 Chart correction
4 Dead reckoning and estimated position	1 Definition of DR and EP 2 Working up DR and EP by plotting on a chart
5 The position line	1 Sources of position lines
6 The magnetic compass	1 Allowance for variation; change of variation with time and position 2 Siting of compass and causes of deviation 3 Deviation, allowance for 4 Steering and hand bearing compasses 5 Swing for deviation (but not correction)
7 Position fixing	1 Techniques of visual fixing 2 Horizontal angle fixing 3 Running fixes 4 Radio fixes

	5 Fixes containing a mixture of position lines
	6 Derivation of position from a line of soundings
	7 Ranges by dipping distances
8 Basic coastal navigation	1 Routine for navigating a yacht in coastal waters
	2 Strategy of course laying
9 Tides	1 Causes of tides – springs and neaps
	2 Tide tables – Admiralty and almanacs
	3 Tidal levels and data
	4 Times and heights at standard ports
	5 The rule of twelfths
	6 Corrections for secondary ports
	7 Tidal anomalies (Solent, etc)
10 Tidal streams	1 Tidal stream atlas
	2 Tidal diamonds
	3 Tidal stream information in sailing directions and yachtsmen's almanacs
	4 Allowance for tidal streams in computing a course to steer
	5 Tide rips, overfalls and races
	6 Tidal stream observation by buoys, beacons, etc
11 Buoyage	1 IALA System A
	2 Limitations of buoys as navigational aids
12 Lights	1 Characteristics
	2 Ranges – visual, luminous and nominal ranges
	3 Light lists – Admiralty and almanacs
13 Pilotage	1 Harbour regulations and control signals
	2 Method of pre-planning
	3 Clearing lines
14 Echo sounders and lead line	1 Principle of operation
	2 Types available – rotating neon, dial and pointer, recording

xiii

	3	Reduction of soundings
	4	'Second trace' echoes
	5	Marking of lead line
15 Radio direction finding	1	Radio beacons, ALRS Vol II and almanacs
	2	D/F receivers, types of aerials; method of operation; audio and visual null points; reciprocal bearings
16 Logs (speed and distance measuring)	1	Types and principles of operation; comparison of the following types:
		(a) towed
		(b) pressure
		(c) impeller
17 Deck log	1	Importance of log as yacht's official document
	2	Layout of log; hourly and occasional entries
18 Meteorology	1	Basic met. terms; the Beaufort scale
	2	Air masses
	3	Cloud types
	4	Weather patterns associated with pressure and frontal systems
	5	Weather forecasts and simple met. instruments
	6	Ability to sketch a weather map from a shipping forecast
	7	Land and sea breezes
	8	Sea fog – forecasting
19 Anchoring	1	Types of anchors and principles of operation
	2	Selection of an anchor berth
20 Rule of the road	1	A sound knowledge of the International Regulations for Preventing Collisions at Sea, except Annexes 1 and 3
21 Safety at sea	1	Personal safety; use of lifejacket; safety harnesses and lifelines
	2	Fire prevention and fire fighting

xiv

	3	Distress signals
	4	Coastguards
	5	First aid; contents of first aid kit; prevention and treatment of likely accidents and seasickness
	6	Action to be taken in heavy weather

22 Signals

1 Ability to recognize morse symbols for letters and numerals by light and sound, and to transmit morse symbols by light
2 Ability to recognize alphabetical flags and numeral pennants of the International Code of Signals
3 Knowledge of the use of urgent and important meanings of single letters
4 The law and customs relating to flags
5 Procedures for VHF radiotelephone working for intership, port operations, distress, urgency and safety

23 Navigation in restricted visibility

1 Precautions to be taken in fog
2 Limitations to safe navigation imposed by fog

24 Passage planning and making

1 Preparation of charts and notebook for route planning and use at sea
2 Customs regulations as they apply to yachts
3 M notices

SIGNALS

The signals section of the Yachtmaster course is among the most straightforward, although it does require a bit of serious swotting which some students may not have faced since leaving school.

Fortunately, even if you have never attempted to learn the Morse Code, let alone clicked away with an Aldis lamp, you will probably find that you know a few of the letters: maybe SOS $\cdots---\cdots$; or V $\cdots-$ for victory and Beethoven's fifth symphony; or perhaps the single dot of the letter E, the most frequently used in the alphabet, and familiar as the sound signal ships use when they are turning to starboard; in which case you have also come across the letter I, two dots, meaning 'I am directing my course to port'; and if you think of Morse as the 'dot dash' code, as some people do, that is appropriately the first symbol, for the letter A. In this way you can tick off six of the letters, about 20 per cent of the alphabet, before you really start.

The same will be true when you take a first look at the flags of the International Code of Signals. You may well have had occasion to hoist the simple yellow square of the letter Q on returning from a foreign cruise, indicating to the Customs men that 'My vessel is healthy and I request free pratique' – or just that you want to get ashore as quickly as possible with the duty-free wine. The 'Blue Peter' of letter P – a blue flag with a small white square in the middle – may be familiar from racing start lines, or for its traditional meaning that 'All persons should report on board as the vessel is about to proceed to sea'. Or perhaps you recall using the blue and yellow stripes of the G flag – 'I require a pilot' – and also recognize the pilot's red and white flag, reflecting the distinguishing lights shown at the pilot cutter's masthead.

With even a few landmarks – or seamarks – of this sort already in mind, it will be easier to arrange the rest of the code in your memory. Incidentally to have learnt and half forgotten them many years ago – before prosaic Anglo Saxon Roger was displaced in the phonetic alphabet by cosmopolitan Romeo, for example – may not be the advantage it seems. The symbols of the Morse Code have not changed over the years, but some of the single letter meanings, whether signalled by Morse or flag, have been altered. For instance the J flag no longer informs other seafarers that 'I am going to send a message by semaphore' – nor are modern yachtmasters expected to be able to do such a thing.

The Yachtmaster Offshore course *does* require:

(i) the ability to recognize the Morse symbols for letters and numerals by light and sound (that is, signalled either with a flashing light or a telegraphic buzzer) and to transmit Morse symbols by light

(ii) the ability to recognize the alphabetical flags and numeral pennants (a pennant is long and tapered as opposed to roughly square) of the International Code of Signals

(iii) knowledge of the use of urgent and important meanings of single letters

(iv) knowledge of the law and customs relating to flags

(v) knowledge of VHF radiotelephone procedure

How you approach this syllabus and exactly how you are tested on it will depend on your instructor. But he will certainly expect you to know all the letter flags and their single meanings (all of them officially defined as 'very urgent') plus the substitute flags that are used when hoisting a longer flag signal – and do not forget the numeral pennants because the examiner may hope to catch you out with them. He will also expect you to read a simple group of Morse letters and transmit one back to him, however slowly.

Once you really know the Morse Code, it is surprisingly easy to develop some sort of slow rhythm on a buzzer, a rhythm, incidentally, which is said by radio men to be as characteristic of an individual as a fingerprint. As for the problem of memorizing the symbols in the first place, everyone will have their own little mental tricks.

The instructor may start with some of the more familiar letters, as we have suggested, and build round them. He may take them in consecutive groups, week by week. Either way it is most useful to have a complete set of symbols, flags and meanings, pasted up on a card that can be slipped into your briefcase for surreptitious swotting on the train home; or perhaps better still a series of individual cards, one for each letter (and on good quality cardboard, because they get a lot of handling), that can be shuffled through whenever you have a spare moment and later extended to include the lights and shapes you have to learn from Part C of the International Maritime Organisation's collision regulations. The Morse numerals are probably best learnt as a complete group, because they make a logical visual pattern.

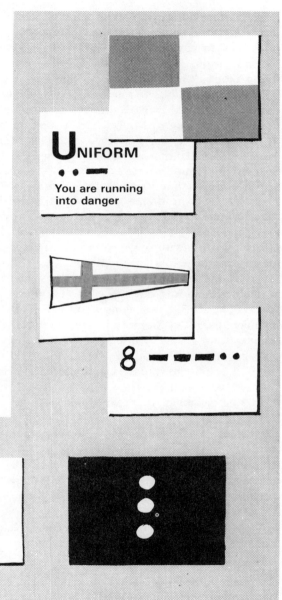

How to learn signals. Write and draw on cards signals from the Morse Code, International Code of Signals and Collision Regulations.

Two other dodges the authors found helpful were to learn some of the letters in similar pairs, and to make up a set of mnemonics. For example if the Morse letter A is written ·– , then the letter N is A backwards –· ; D –·· is a mirror image of U ··– ; and E · pairs neatly with T – . The important thing about a Morse mnemonic is that it should convey the rhythm as well as the identity of the letter, as in 'God save the Queen' ––·– for the letter Q. One we particularly like, for its echoes of Messiah, and attributed by *Yachting Monthly* to Mr Michael Young, is 'King of Kings' –·– for the letter K. And if you find this approach helps you learn the symbols, something similar may work for the meanings – 'yanking' up the anchor, for instance, to remind yourself that Y –·–– means 'I am dragging my anchor'.

Once you begin to string Morse letters together, you will find it preferable to adopt the professionals' habit of talking about 'dit dah' rather than 'dot dash', because again it conveys the essential rhythm much better. The RYA has produced two excellent tapes from which you can practise reading Morse, starting with single letters, slowly repeated, and gradually building up to a complete message at full speed.

When the examination is over you may want to invest in an Aldis signalling lamp and develop your new found skill. Other yachtsmen are always impressed by someone who can actually use Morse in a professional manner at sea. But for most people, we suspect, memory begins to fade the moment they walk out of the examination room and the practical objective may be limited to retaining:

 (i) the ability to read the identifying Morse characteristics transmitted by radio beacons
 (ii) the meanings of at least a dozen of the most important single letter signals

Thames Estuary sailors will obviously want to recognize the radio signal of the North Foreland lighthouse, NF –· ··–· ; those sailing in the Solent will think in terms of the Nab Tower, NB –· –··· . The single letter meanings can be conveyed either by flashing light or flag (or by sound, provided you do not contravene the collision regulations). For a complete list of signals, see page 50.

Flags and flag etiquette provide a colourful link between modern yachting and the long traditions of the Royal Navy and the Merchant Marine. The

---

Throughout the book on the bottom left-hand corner of most pages you will find symbols and signals for self testing, with answers on the facing page.

four main flags (other than signal flags) which concern yachtsmen are the ensign, the burgee, the courtesy flag and the racing flag.

The burgee is a triangular flag flown, or worn, at the mainmast head. This flag shows your vessel is a yacht. It should only be worn when the owner is on board or nearby and it indicates by its design and colour the yacht club to which he belongs. Club commodores may fly special flags of the same pattern, but square shaped with a swallow tail, called broad pennants. A vice-commodore has a similar swallow tail with one ball in the fly; a rear-commodore has two balls thus shown. A club 'admiral' or president has a rectangular flag. Sailing yachts which belong to no club nevertheless wear burgees to indicate the wind direction.

The ensign distinguishes a vessel's nationality. It should be worn by day, in the after part of the vessel — that is, on its own staff at the stern, from a backstay, from the peak of a gaff sail, or at the mizzen masthead. Any British yacht may wear the red ensign, coloured red with the union flag in the upper canton — that is, the corner from which it is hoisted. The red ensign is also worn by most British merchant ships.

Some yacht clubs are granted an ensign warrant entitling members' yachts to wear the blue ensign, which is normally flown only by vessels belonging to government departments. The yachts concerned must be registered, of more than two tons and have an individually issued warrant. Such an ensign, blue coloured with the union flag in the upper canton, may be 'defaced' by the club's badge, as may red ensigns which are also the subject of an individual warrant.

The White Ensign, coloured white with the red cross of St George and the union flag in the same upper corner, is worn only by ships of the Royal Navy and yachts belonging to members of the Royal Yacht Squadron.

To salute a passing vessel, especially a warship of any nationality, the ensign is partially lowered, or 'dipped', until the other vessel has lowered and rehoisted her own — a traditional maritime courtesy, but one to be used sparingly unless you are prepared sometimes to be snubbed by not having it returned.

When visiting a foreign port, it is considered courteous to fly the ensign of that country at the crosstrees. A British vessel of any kind must also wear her own flags, or colours.

A rectangular racing flag, to any pattern the owner fancies, is often worn in place of the burgee to show that a sailing yacht is racing — and that her crew will appreciate being left clear to manoeuvre in a clean wind, although the collision regulations still apply. This flag should be hauled down and

Romeo

replaced when the race ends or the yacht retires from it. Owing to masthead fittings such as wind indicators and VHF aerials, the racing flag is less and less seen. The RYA prescribes in its racing rules that an ensign shall not be worn when racing. An ensign does therefore signal that a boat is not racing: lack of one, of course, does not indicate that she is.

The customs on club burgees and racing flags are not observed outside Britain and decreasingly so by British yachts.

VHF radio

The traditional methods of communicating at sea, by lights and flags, continue to be immensely important and are treated as such in the Yachtmaster course. But an increasing number of yachts are being fitted with VHF (Very High Frequency) radiotelephones and since 1980 the RYA has recognized this by including a working knowledge of radio procedure among its requirements.

A band of VHF frequencies is allocated under an international agreement for use by ships or yachts, and divided into a large number of channels, or specific frequencies. Each channel is in turn allocated to a specific function – for distress calls, intership calls, port operations and so on.

For example, Channel 16 (156.8 MHz) is both the VHF international distress frequency and the calling channel on which most other calls are initiated before switching to a working channel, so as to leave it clear for other traffic. Channel 16 is therefore mandatory on even the smallest VHF set. So is Channel 6 – the main intership working channel. Many of the coastal radio stations work on Channels 24 to 28, Channels 12 and 14 are often used for port control, and Channel 67 has been specially allocated in the UK to enable small craft and the Coastguard to exchange safety information.

The point about VHF as opposed to MF (Medium Frequency) radio is that it is virtually limited to 'line-of-sight' ranges, say about 10 miles from one yacht to another, or about 50 miles when talking to a coastal radio station. But this limitation gives the paradoxical advantage that a lot of scattered craft can use the same frequency without getting in one another's way. Once in contact, VHF reception is likely to be clear; the equipment is relatively cheap and the drain on your batteries small.

The basic radiotelephone typically fitted on yachts uses the same aerial to transmit and receive, so you cannot speak and listen at the same time as in normal conversation. In other words the set is limited to simplex operation, in which each transmission ends with the characteristic radio word 'over' to let the other person know it is their turn to speak. But other sets are designed for duplex two-way conversation on working channels provided with two frequencies for this purpose.

All radio operators develop their own jargon and procedure, to speed communication and remove ambiguities. The marine fraternity are no exception and although it may sound rather artificial at first, using the phonetic alphabet, repeating key words with the introductory phrase 'I say again', turning the number nine into 'niner', and so on, it has evolved from long practical experience (the proper words can be found in the Department of Trade's Standard Marine Navigational Vocabulary). Chatting may be permissible between trawlermen, or while you are telephoning your wife to say when you expect to make harbour, but the general rule is to say what you have to say in the concise, standard form and get off the air.

Many of the rules — such as allowing a coastal radio station to control communications because of its longer effective range — are common sense. The full VHF procedure is laid out in the RYA's pamphlet G 22, which instructors will no doubt advise you to read before tackling exercise questions. The basics can be illustrated in a couple of examples.

Imagine the yacht *Touchstone* running down the Yorkshire coast and wanting to call someone ashore. Her operator switches to Channel 16, checks it is clear, and transmits:

WHITBY RADIO, WHITBY RADIO. THIS IS *TOUCHSTONE*. CAN I HAVE A LINK CALL PLEASE? OVER.

After a moment, if she is lucky, *Touchstone* hears the coastal station reply:

HELLO *TOUCHSTONE*. THIS IS WHITBY RADIO. CHANNEL 25. STAND BY. OVER.

The yacht's operator acknowledges:

HELLO WHITBY. THIS IS *TOUCHSTONE*, CHANNEL 25. GOING NOW. OVER.

When Whitby Radio is ready to handle the call her operator comes back on the working frequency Channel 25:

HELLO *TOUCHSTONE*. THIS IS WHITBY RADIO. PLEASE GIVE ME YOUR CALL SIGN AND SPELL YOUR VESSEL'S NAME. OVER.

The yacht replies:

WHITBY. *TOUCHSTONE*. MY CALL SIGN IS MIKE NOVEMBER ZULU QUEBEC. I SPELL *TOUCHSTONE* T-O-U-C-H-S-T-O-N-E. OVER.

Hotel

Whitby Radio replies:

TOUCHSTONE. THIS IS WHITBY RADIO. WHAT NUMBER DO YOU WANT? OVER.

The yacht gives the dialling code and number she wants ashore, and stands by until connected. Note the unambiguous identifying words 'This is', the phonetic call sign, and the simplex requirement for 'over' each time. At the end of the call Whitby will give *Touchstone* the time and cost of her call, and the conversation closes on both sides with the word 'out'.

Further south next morning, the yacht *Shanty* is in serious trouble, on fire off the Norfolk coast. She uses Channel 16 to send out a Mayday international distress call:

MAYDAY, MAYDAY, MAYDAY. THIS IS *SHANTY, SHANTY, SHANTY.* MAYDAY *SHANTY* FIVE MILES EAST OF CROMER. I SAY AGAIN FIVE MILES EAST OF CROMER. FIRE OUT OF CONTROL. WILL ABANDON YACHT FOR INFLATABLE AND FIRE ROCKETS. OVER.

Note the repetition of the MAYDAY [derived from the French *m'aidez*] and the vitally important position, which should normally be given as a true bearing and distance from a known object. *Touchstone*, by now coasting past Sea Palling, not so far away, hears the distress call. But like a couple of other nearby vessels, she has the good sense to wait a few moments before acknowledging receipt of the MAYDAY in case Bacton Radio, or perhaps Yarmouth Coastguard, have also heard it. In any case she heads for the position indicated and judges her moment to tell *Shanty* – if her operator is still there to listen – when she expects to arrive. If necessary, she may also relay *Shanty*'s brief call:

MAYDAY RELAY, MAYDAY RELAY, MAYDAY RELAY. THIS IS *TOUCHSTONE, TOUCHSTONE, TOUCHSTONE.* MAYDAY *SHANTY* FIVE MILES EAST OF CROMER. FIRE OUT OF CONTROL. CREW ABANDONING YACHT FOR INFLATABLE AND FIRING ROCKETS. I AM PROCEEDING TO HER POSITION, ESTIMATING ARRIVAL AT 1200. OVER.

If *Shanty* had been in less serious trouble, disabled perhaps, but not in 'grave and imminent danger, requiring immediate assistance', she might have sent out an urgency signal to all stations, preceded by the words PAN PAN, giving her position and specifying the assistance needed.

Note also that yachts may carry emergency-only transmitters, broadcasting on the MF distress frequency 2182 kHz, or the aircraft frequencies 121.5 and 243 MHz.

NAVIGATION

Navigation is the art of moving safely across the sea by relating information about the yacht's position to a chart of that area. As far as this course is concerned, the main sources of that information are:

   (i) any buoys, seamarks or coastal features that are visible

  (ii) the magnetic compass, which gives the bearing of objects you can see or of radio beacons you can hear, plus the direction you are steering

 (iii) the log, showing speed and distance

 (iv) the echo sounder or lead line, both of which measure the depth of water

This section of the book deals with these and other navigational subjects covered by the Yachtmaster assessment papers, though not necessarily in quite the same order.

The offshore racing yachtsman likes to know precisely where he is at all times. The cruising man can afford to take things a bit easier, provided he anticipates the occasions when he really does need an accurate position – winding his way through sandbanks on a falling tide, for instance, or making a landfall in bad visibility. In practice, therefore, navigational techniques range all the way from the crumpled-chart-on-the-cockpit-seat school right through to the pedantic style that expects a course to be plotted from the marina berth to the harbour pierheads. But the would-be yachtmaster should err on the side of pedantry.

The RYA's introductory notes have admitted that the standards of accuracy demanded in its theoretical classroom exercises – and carefully defined – are rarely obtainable in a small boat at sea. But the notes also argued that a mathematically correct calculation is nevertheless the best starting point for any subsequent guesswork. More to the point, it's what the examiners require, and therefore the best way to pass your Yachtmaster's.

The chart

Like land maps, charts are the projection of a curved surface on to a flat

Uniform

sheet of paper. The common projection is Mercator's. This involves spreading out the lines of longitude, measured in degrees east or west of the Greenwich meridian, so they are drawn parallel instead of converging at the poles, as they do on a globe. But to maintain the shape of the coastline, the lines of latitude, measured in degrees from the Equator, also have to be spread out as you move north or south. This is why distances should be measured along the side of the chart at the latitude which is roughly level with the yacht's position.

One minute of latitude – a sixtieth of a degree – is a nautical mile and it averages out (because the earth is not exactly spherical) at 6076 feet or 1852 metres. A cable is a tenth of a nautical mile, roughly 200 yards.

On charts drawn from Mercator's projection – which means most of them – a straight line, or rhumb line, is not the shortest distance between two real points. That would be a great circle, which appears on the chart as a curved line. This rarely matters to yachtsmen. However some charts do show the lines of longitude converging as they would on a globe, using a Gnomonic projection, so that the shortest distance between two points can be drawn conveniently as a straight line.

British charts are drawn from surveys conducted by the Royal Navy's hydrographic department and similar foreign organizations with which it exchanges data. The Admiralty publishes its own comprehensive series of charts, details of which are given in the *Catalogue of Admiralty Charts and other Hydrographic Publications* (and in a useful abbreviated catalogue covering only the British Isles and adjacent continental waters).

Admiralty charts set the standard, but there are other more limited series, published by Imray and Stanfords especially for yachtsmen, which are in some ways more useful aboard a small boat. The Admiralty series is naturally designed primarily for use by large merchant vessels and warships. Most of the charts are large – as are many of the yachting variety – but they do not come ready folded into a handy 'concertina'. They are intended to be laid out in a wheelhouse on a full-sized chart table, not stuffed into a transparent plastic cover so the helmsman can do his own pilotage in a damp cockpit.

The yachting charts make more use of colour, for example to indicate the red, green and white sectors of a lighthouse. In general the information they show is selected with small vessels in mind, not container ships or supertankers. There are harbour plans, tidal streams on miniature charts (rather than as a list of compass bearings and speeds), pilotage tips for approaching river entrances, and so on.

One thing you need to know about any chart is whether it is up to date. On Admiralty charts the basic date of the edition is shown in the lower margin on the right hand side and the date of correction on the bottom left. Other charts use a similar notation. But of course changes do not stop when you buy the chart. If you want to keep it right up to date you need to check through the weekly *Notices to Mariners*, which are available at chart agents or through the post. Some of the yachting magazines reproduce them and there is also a special *Small Craft Edition* of the notices, published quarterly, and covering just UK and near continental waters.

The traditional unit of depth at sea is the fathom – 6 feet. But like other traditional measurements it is slowly giving way to the process of metrication. The hydrographer is steadily working through his 3000 charts changing from one system to the other, and while he is about it, introducing a bit more colour and changing some of the symbols and abbreviations to conform with international practice. At the time of writing, therefore, the student yachtmaster is expected to be familiar with both systems, but fortunately much of the notation is common to both.

Each chart says clearly whether soundings are in feet, fathoms or metres. In shallower areas tenths of a metre, or feet in the case of fathom charts, are shown by smaller figures alongside the main depth markings. Drying heights above low water are underlined.

A complete list of the *Symbols and Abbreviations used on Admiralty Charts* is published as *Chart No 5011*, now available in book form. There are thousands of these symbols and abbreviations. But many are self evident, like the little drawings of buoys with their various topmarks. Others, such as the symbol for lava flowing down the side of a volcano, can safely be ignored. In any case this is a subject, like safety equipment and navigational aids, where students have been encouraged to consult references when doing the assessment papers (whereas those dealing with meteorology, collision regulations and navigational calculation have been done under examination conditions).

Perhaps the best way to acquire a useful knowledge, other than by simply working with charts, is to learn at least the main symbols and abbreviations in a few important categories. Ways of marking wrecks and dangerous rocks are an obvious example. So are the abbreviations for different kinds of seabed – S for sand, M for mud and so on – and the descriptions of light characteristics.

On a metric chart, a small lighthouse might be annotated as Fl(2)WRG.10s14m7-5M. This means that its light flashes twice every ten

Thunder

seconds; it has three fixed sectors showing white, red and green; it stands 14 metres above high water on a spring tide; and the luminous range of its multi-coloured light is from seven to five nautical miles (note the possible confusion between lower case m for metres and upper case M for miles). The luminous range of a light is the distance it can be seen in clear visibility – which is also the nominal range when 'clear' visibility is defined as 10 miles. The geographical range is the distance at which the light can be seen above the horizon from a height of 15 feet above the sea – as you might have been on an old sailing ship. One of the fascinations of a powerful lighthouse from seaward is that the loom of its rotating beam can often be seen before its light rises above the horizon.

On an older, fathom chart, a light might be described as Alt.Fl.WR.30s 100ft21/20M – meaning that it flashes alternately white and red in a 30-second sequence, stands 100 feet above high water, and has a range of 20 to 21 miles.

Where light buoys are concerned, some of the older forms of abbreviation are more explicit than the standard international forms. The description Int V Qk Fl (interrupted very quick flash), for instance, is surely easier to understand than just IVQ. Either way you need to be familiar with most of them and especially those associated with the new buoyage introduced into European waters by the International Association of Lighthouse Authorities (IALA System A).

Some commonly used symbols and abbreviations

Wk	wreck
	wreck showing at very low water
	wreck considered dangerous (coloured blue on Admiralty charts)
	wreck over which depth, as shown, has been sounded
+++	wreck not considered dangerous
	rock awash at very low water
+	rock barely covered or otherwise dangerous
	overfalls or tide rip
	underwater cable
S	sand
M	mud
Sn	shingle
Sh	shells

R	red
G	green
W	white
F	fixed (steady light)
Fl	flashing (single light flashes)
L Fl	long flashing (flashes of at least 2 seconds)
Fl(3) *or* Gp Fl(3)	groups of three flashes
Q *or* Qk Fl	continuous quick flashing – as fitted on N cardinal buoys
Q(3) *or* Qk Fl(3)	groups of three quick flashes – as fitted on E cardinal buoys
IQ *or* Int Qk Fl	interrupted quick flashing
VQ *or* V Qk Fl	continuous very quick flashing – as fitted on N cardinal buoys
VQ(3) *or* V Qk Fl(3)	groups of three very quick flashes – as fitted on E cardinal buoys
IVQ *or* Int V Qk Fl	interrupted very quick flashing
Oc *or* Occ	occulting (only short periods of darkness) – indicating safe water
Iso	isophase (equal periods of light and darkness) – indicating safe water
dia	diaphone (low pitched fog signal ending in 'grunt')
reed	reed (higher pitched fog signal)
⚓	anchorage

The IALA buoyage system

Navigational buoys are distinguished by shape, colour, and the light they show. Their arrangement follows two main principles – lateral and cardinal (see plate 2).

In a lateral system, as used until recently in British waters, buoys are laid to port and starboard of the navigable water according to what is known as the conventional direction of buoyage – which now runs mainly from SW to NE round the British Isles and then into the various estuaries and rivers. This method lends itself to buoying a clearly defined channel especially in an estuary, like the Thames, where the conventional direction is also the direction of the flood tide and the way into port.

In a cardinal system, formerly associated with continental waters, buoys

Victor

are distinguished according to the cardinal points of the compass – N, E, S and W – and placed in that direction from the point of interest or danger they mark. This method is particularly suitable for marking, say, the edges of an offshore sandbank or a coastal reef, although it can also be used to mark the features of a channel.

IALA System A, which is already established round the British Isles and scheduled for introduction throughout NW Europe by the mid 1980s, combines both the lateral and cardinal principles – port and starboard marks for channels and cardinal ones mainly for other features. When the first buoys were laid in 1977 there was a certain amount of scepticism. Seafarers tend to be traditionalists. But in fact the new system has many advantages and listing them makes it easier to understand how and why it was evolved.

For a start it sets a European standard, so that although its rules may look complicated at first sight, once learnt there are relatively few local variations. It also allows the pilotage authorities – primarily Trinity House in the case of Britain – to choose the best type of marking for the job. This has incidentally meant the introduction in British waters of rather more tall pillar buoys with a 'high focal plane', which in clear weather are easier to spot from the yachtsman's poor vantage point just above the sea – or nearly in it! Another plus is that red and green channel buoys are consistently to port and starboard where they match a ship's navigation lights.

The lighting of the buoys is unambiguous. Lateral channel buoys have appropriate red or green lights, and can be made to flash in a variety of rhythms to distinguish one from another because their basic navigational message is conveyed by the colour. Cardinal marks have white lights, flashing to different rhythms according to the quadrant of the compass they represent.

One of the few features the IALA system does not offer is a special colour for wreck marks – which used to be green. But, as the 1971 Channel pile-up near the Varne light vessel showed, indicating the direction in which a dangerous wreck lies – something a cardinal buoy does well – may be even more important than simply indicating that it is a wreck. That particular series of casualties led to an additional feature of IALA A, the doubling of marks to indicate a new danger.

Green lights, which the new system uses more frequently, have a shorter range of visibility than red or white ones. But that is a small loss compared with the simplicity of leaving green buoys to starboard when inbound along a channel. One colour problem yachtsmen have commented upon is the difficulty of distinguishing the black and yellow bands on the steel lat-ticework of cardinal pillar buoys. This matters less if the distinguishing topmarks, which convey the same message, are of a decent size.

If you are learning the system from scratch, note that the conical north and south cardinal topmarks point in the appropriate compass direction (compare the north and south gale warning cones). Thinking of the westerly topmark as a wineglass, or of the easterly one as an egg, may help to fix them in the memory. As for the light characteristics, notice that they are arranged in a clockwise sequence – continuous single flashing for north, three flashes for east, six for south (plus the distinguishing long flash), and nine for west. You will see that the traditional principle of conical shaped buoys to starboard and flat topped can buoys to port is retained as an option in both the lateral marks and the special marks used for traffic separation schemes, spoil grounds and so on.

In the assessment paper on pilotage and visual aids (not necessarily done under examination conditions), students are expected to identify various buoys by their shapes and light characteristics, bearing in mind that a 'quick' flashing light flashes about once a second, and a 'very quick' flash is twice a second. An occulting light (compare the occluded front in meteor-ology) remains lit for most of the time, with only short periods of darkness – in other words the reverse of a flashing light. The description isophase (compare isobar) means that the periods of light and dark are equal. Notice that these last two characteristics are both associated with safety in the IALA system.

Three other points worth remembering about buoys: they have to have a fair scope of mooring chain to cope with the tidal range, so their position can never be absolutely precise; they make excellent tidal stream indicators; and if you are not sure of their identity, or what they signify, it may be safest to sail right up to them.

The magnetic compass

There are 32 points on a full compass rose, each measuring 11¼° of the circle. But on a modern yacht steering compass only 8 points are usually marked – N, NE, E, SE and so on. The primary marking is in degrees from 0 to 360, usually at intervals of 5°. This is about the smallest margin of error you can hope for in steering a sailing boat, although on the chart you lay a course to the nearest degree.

The course is held by keeping some sort of fore and aft lubber line against

Fog

the required mark on the compass card, or by setting an adjustable steering grid on top of the compass card on the chosen course and then lining up the compass needle – and hence the boat – with it. A grid design might just be usable at night with only luminous paint but most compasses are lit either by a small conventional bulb or by a fluorescent Beta light.

The traditional compass card is read from above, but some compasses are designed for mounting in a vertical bulkhead or at eye level on top of a coachroof, and these can be read from the side. The important thing is to position the compass as far as possible from the magnetic interference of the ferrous metals that are always present in a boat's engine, in her keel if of iron, and in various fittings round the cockpit. Electrical equipment like radios and echo sounders should also be avoided.

But however carefully it is sited, the compass needle is almost bound to show some deviation from the magnetic pole, if only by a few degrees one way or the other. A big deviation can be roughly checked by comparison with a hand bearing compasses held well away from possible interference. This deviation will vary with the boat's heading, so accurate navigation – and the yachtmaster's chartwork – demand the use of a deviation card, showing the error in degrees E or W for every couple of compass points, or better still a curve on which the error associated with any given course can be interpolated. Preparing an accurate card for your own boat is a complicated procedure that involves turning her slowly through successive headings while checking the steering compass against the known bearing of a distant object – or building up a card as opportunities arise during the season. But for the Yachtmaster's a standard deviation table is provided in the course notes.

Compass work also involves a more fundamental allowance for the variation between the direction of the magnetic pole and true north, as shown by the lines of longitude on a normal Mercator chart. The compass

Although some charts for yachtsmen only have magnetic north marked on the compass rose, in the examination you are expected to take account of the variation between magnetic and true north. The magnetic variation for one area can be considered constant – unlike the deviation of the compass needle caused by ferrous metal and electrical fields on board, which alters with every heading and can be either east or west. The upper diagram should help you to fix this basic principle in your mind. The destination is true north but both the magnetic variation and compass deviation are pulling the compass needle west. In the lower diagram variation and deviation are pulling in opposite directions.

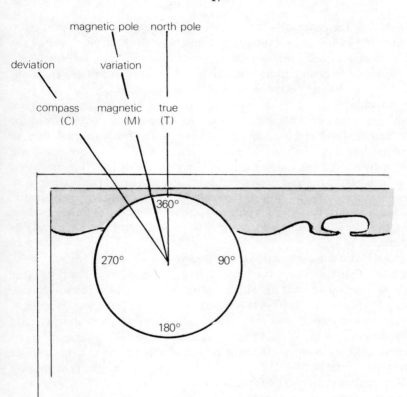

If your true course is 085° and variation is pulling the compass needle 6° to the West and deviation pulling it back 2° East, your compass course would be 089°

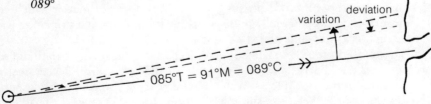

Mike

rose printed on the chart is usually in fact two roses, one inside the other, to give both true bearings or courses, and magnetic ones. In our part of the world, a compass needle points to the west of true north. In the North Sea, for example, the present variation is about 6°W, slowly decreasing by about 4' a year but as distance is covered, so the variation changes.

It is possible to navigate entirely with magnetic bearings and courses, using the inner ring of the compass rose. The information coming from the yacht's steering and hand bearing compasses is in this form after all. But the chart grid is laid out on a true basis and much of the other information you will need, for example tidal streams, is likely to be presented in the same way. So whichever way you prefer to work, the problem of converting from compass bearings to true and back again is going to arise – and in the navigational classroom it occurs only too often. One of the first things to get straight, therefore, is some foolproof way of remembering and checking this procedure.

If you look at a compass rose, you will see that with 6° westerly variation, a magnetic bearing is always that many degrees more than its true equivalent. True north lines up with 6° magnetic (0T=6M), true south lines up with 186° magnetic (180T=186M) and so on. The same would apply if the compass difference was a combination of westerly variation and westerly deviation – say 6° variation plus 2° deviation – a total of 8° to be subtracted from the compass bearing (which in this case is not the same as the magnetic bearing) to make it true. The true south might now line up with 188° on the compass (180T=188C).

If the error is east on the other hand, either an easterly deviation on its own or a large deviation of, say, 8° combined with 6° westerly variation to leave a net error of 2°E, then the opposite rule will apply. The 2° must be added to convert a compass reading to true.

There are various tricks and mnemonics for remembering all this. For example we have used the letters ADDECT (add easterly compass to true). Your instructor will no doubt suggest others. It does not matter which you choose. But unless you really prefer working it out from first principles each time, find one that suits and stick to it.

To find the compass bearing of an object from your boat, so that you can plot it on the chart, it may be possible to use a suitably placed steering compass. But most people use a small hand bearing compass, with a special sight, that can be held in a suitable position clear of magnetic interference. And if this is combined with a small radio set that has a directional aerial, you have the makings of a primitive radio direction finding instrument.

Radio direction finding

If you had the room and the power supply on board for all the radio and radar aids that are available these days you would have a fair chance of getting from one port to another without ever leaving the chart table to look outside. There are complete position finding systems like Decca and Loran, coastal radio direction finding (RDF) stations which will tell a ship her bearing from that station, directional radio beacons that will lead you into port, and aeronautical radio beacons, some of which are also useful at sea. But the aid most familiar to yachtsmen is the simple omnidirectional marine radio beacon from which you can take a bearing with an RDF set little more sophisticated than the combination of compass and radio receiver mentioned above.

The basic principle is that each radio beacon broadcasts an identifying Morse signal at a given frequency of around 300 kHz – that is at one end of the long wave band of any radio receiver. The North Foreland signal is NF —· ··—· on 301.1 kHz; the Nab Tower, NB —· —··· on 312.6 kHz and so on. This is one practical reason for the work you put in learning the Morse Code.

Receivers are of two main types – those having ferrite rod aerials which receive best when at right angles to the signal and those with loop aerials which need to be lined up with the signal to achieve the same effect. But paradoxically, the bearing is actually taken by rotating the aerial to find the null at which the aerial is 'wrongly' aligned so the signal cannot be heard through your earphones, because this is quite a sharply defined point. The recommended technique is to swing the aerial backwards and forwards across the null to close in gradually on the bearing.

Steel boats, which cannot operate a receiver inside the hull, may have a loop aerial mounted in the cabin roof, from which a relative bearing can be taken to compare with the steering compass. But the sets most commonly found aboard yachts use some combination of the ferrite rod aerial, compass and receiver, often in one portable unit. The rapid advance of electronics means that more expensive sets incorporate all sorts of extras such as digital tuning, visual indication of the null or even a pointer which shows you where the beacon lies.

To reduce radio interference and make things easier for the navigator, many of the beacons use the same frequency, in groups of up to six often quite close to one another. For example one group at the southern entrance to the North Sea consists of the Falls, Tongue and West Hinder light vessels, the Ostend rear lighthouse, plus the Dunkerque and East Goodwin light

Golf

vessels. They take it in turns to broadcast their identifying signal in a sequence that lasts six minutes however many there are in the group. The navigator does not have to retune and provided he can hear several of the stations he can rapidly fix his position.

Radio bearings are not necessarily accurate. Just as a compass may show deviation, a radio bearing may suffer from quadrantal error – the distortion caused especially by closed loops of metal rigging (one reason for fixing wire guardrails with rope lanyards). A new RDF set therefore has to be visually calibrated just as you check a compass for deviation.

Another source of error is the night effect – the reflected signals from the ionosphere, especially prevalent at longer ranges from about an hour before sunset to an hour after sunrise, which make the null indistinct. Signals passing over a coastline at a shallow angle tend to be refracted, or bent, in towards the land. This is one reason why aeronautical beacons situated inland may be unsuitable for marine use although they do have the convenience of continuous transmission. Finally, bearings may be unreliable at night if the beacon is more than about 25 miles away or beyond its officially quoted range.

The log

As its name implies, this piece of navigational equipment started as a wooden 'log chip' thrown over the stern to see how fast the knots marking its line ran out. Nowadays it comes in many exotic forms, each with pros and cons that could be the subject of an examination question. Nearly all of them show both the boat's speed in knots (nautical miles an hour) at a given moment and the distance she has covered through the water (which can be converted into an average speed). But it is the second form of information the navigator ultimately needs, to tell him how far he has moved through the water or when he should start looking for a landfall.

The traditional patent log consists of a spinner towed behind the boat on a long line and attached to a dial on the stern which counts the revolutions. The dial converts these into miles and yards, from which an average speed can be derived. It is a well tried method with the advantages of simplicity and reliability, provided the spinner is checked for weed occasionally and its tendency to sink and underread at very low speeds is allowed for.

A mechanical log can also be driven by a small impeller projecting through the hull, where it is perhaps more prone to damage. The impeller is linked to the dial by a stiff rotating wire, rather like the car's speed and mileage instruments.

In electro-mechanical systems an even smaller impeller or paddle wheel creates electrical impulses that are sensed by an electronic counter. The dial can therefore be placed at the chart table or wherever it suits the navigator, but it may be more difficult to place the tiny external driving unit (which can be retracted for cleaning and repair) where it always receives a smooth flow of water under the hull. The electronic trailing log – in effect the traditional patent log adapted to modern technology – avoids this problem by putting the impeller on the end of an electrical cable. The read out can be on the stern or connected below at the chart table.

An electro-magnetic log also projects through the hull (from which the transducer can be retracted). But the skin fitting is almost flush and since there are no moving parts (the transducer merely detects changes in the magnetic field as the water flows past) that particular source of low-speed inaccuracy is eliminated.

Finally there are logs which use the doppler principle. They require no holes in the hull and have no moving parts, but the sensors are difficult to site accurately.

Depth sounding

The traditional method of sounding shallow depths at sea is the lead line – a line marked in fathoms with strips of leather and bunting, attached to a lump of lead hollowed out on the bottom. The proper markings are:

one fathom – one strip of leather

two fathoms – two strips of leather

three fathoms – three strips of leather

five fathoms – a piece of white cloth

seven fathoms – a piece of red cloth

ten fathoms – one piece of leather with a hole in it

thirteen fathoms – a piece of blue bunting

Many people, however, simply make do with an appropriate number of knots.

The lead can be a pleasure to use, but from the deck of a small yacht bouncing through a seaway it can only be cast through a few fathoms of water. Its only obvious advantage over the modern electrically powered echo sounder – unless your battery is run down – is that the hollow in the bottom can be 'armed' with tallow to bring up a sample of the seabed. In the

X-ray

days before radar and radio this was a valuable addition to the navigator's meagre sources of information and it helps to explain the chartmakers' predilection for those little symbols listed earlier (see page 12), showing whether the seabed consists of mud (M), shells (Sh) or shingle (Sn).

Nowadays most people just switch on the echo sounder, which works by measuring how long it takes for an ultrasonic pulse to be reflected back from the seabed. The depth in fathoms or metres may be indicated by the pointer on a dial, but the most familiar display consists of a light emitting diode (LED) mounted on a revolving arm which flashes when the pulse leaves the transducer and again when the echo returns. The first flash is lined up with zero on the depth scale so that the angular distance between the two – which is easy to judge at night without seeing the scale – indicates the depth of water, or to be more accurate the distance between the transducer and the seabed. The sounding pulse may bounce back to the seabed and return to give a fainter second trace echo which should either be ignored or eliminated by reducing the brightness of the LED. Some sailing yachts fit two transducers so that one is more or less vertical even when going hard to windward. With care, transducers can be fitted inside the hull of a GRP boat, without boring a hole, although the instrument's efficiency at great depths may thereby be reduced.

Tides

Tides are caused by the gravitational pull of the moon and, to a lesser extent, the sun. The orbiting moon produces two high tides every day, or to be a little more precise, about every 24 hours 50 minutes – which is why the time of high water is about 50 minutes later each day.

When the moon is full, or new, the sun's gravitational pull is exerted in the same direction. The movement of the water is greater, tidal streams are faster, the tidal level rises higher, and falls lower, than at other times. These are known as spring tides. They occur every two weeks, in keeping with the phases of the moon, and at any given place on the coast, high water will be at roughly the same time of day.

But in alternate weeks, when the sun is pulling at right angles to the moon and partially cancelling out its effect, the tidal range, from high to low water, is smaller. These are called neap tides, less useful if you are trying to float your boat out of a mud berth, but also less of a hazard when crossing a bar at low water. The spring tides, incidentally, are especially high and low during the spring season and in the autumn.

The depths shown on a chart are measured from a level known as the chart datum, which may be either the mean level of low water spring tides (MLWS) or, more commonly these days, the level of the lowest astronomically predictable tide (LAT). The height of a tide is also measured from the chart datum, as is the height of a drying sandbank (the figures underlined on the chart). The height of a lighthouse, on the other hand, is measured from mean high water springs (MHWS) – a point easily forgotten when you are doing an examination question about the distance at which the light will be visible.

At the centre of this oscillating pattern of rising and falling tides is a mean level (ML). This is of more than theoretical importance because some tide tables give the height of high water at a particular port on a particular day, and the mean level, but not the height of low water. Yet because high and low water are equidistant from the mean, the latter can be calculated by taking twice the mean level and subtracting the height of high water.

Definitions of the various tidal levels.

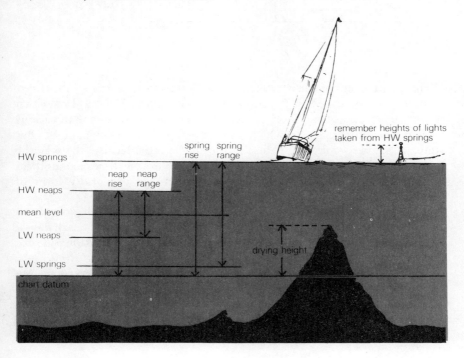

V Qk Fl (3) every 5 sec
or Qk Fl (3) every 10 sec

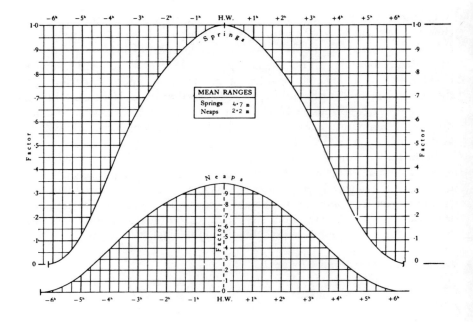

The most comprehensive tidal predictions, and generally the most accurate, are published in the *Admiralty Tide Tables*, Volume I of which covers European waters. There are many others, in almanacs and in various local publications, all of which may have particular advantages. But students are recommended to use the former, partly because the way the information has to be condensed in the other tables sometimes makes them less accurate. More important in this context, the *Admiralty* form of presentation makes it easier to visualize how the tides move.

If you turn, for example, to the *Admiralty* pages dealing with Dover, you will find the times and heights of high and low water laid out for each day of the year (times are in GMT, heights in both feet and metres). Alongside are two graphs or tidal curves – also used, but less extensively, in *Reed's* and *Macmillan's* nautical almanacs with proportional factors marked on the vertical scales and the number of hours before and after high water on the horizontal ones. The factors vary from zero at low tide to 1.0 at high tide.

One curve represents springs and the other neaps, with the average range in metres given in each case. But the curves themselves are not marked in

A curve from Admiralty tide tables and its effect on sea level. The yacht is sailing at 2½ hours after high water. Note that at 3½ hours after HW the shoal would be awash.

metres. They merely show that, for example, on a rising spring tide at Dover, the water will rise by less than a tenth of its eventual range (a factor of less than 0.1) during the first hour (four hours before HW, not five, because in this instance the asymmetrical tide takes less time to rise than it does to fall). After five hours of a falling neap tide, the level will be down to two tenths of the range (a factor of 0.2) and so on.

Similar curves are shown for each of the standard ports. Some curves are quite symmetrical; others are sharply skewed. For ports in the Bristol Channel, where the tidal range is enormous, they are steeply peaked. On the east coast they are much flatter. At Southampton the peak is double, indicating a second high water, because of the curious tidal cycles in the central part of the English Channel.

If you were to take all these individual curves and combine them in a single smooth symmetrical line, that is, the ideal pattern the tide would follow if there were nothing to distort its flow, that line could be expressed as a simple rule: the tide would rise or fall approximately one twelfth of its range in the first hour after low or high water, two twelfths in the second

Lima

hour, three twelfths in the third and fourth hours, two twelfths again in the fifth hour, and one twelfth in the sixth and final hour. So if you find tidal calculations confusing – and let's face it, many fine yachtsmen have no head for figures – remember you can always fall back on this Rule of Twelfths: 1,2,3,3,2,1.

Such a simple pattern will obviously be less accurate than the full calculation on many occasions, especially where the tidal range is large or the rise and fall asymmetrical. But then there are other sources of error in tidal predictions. A rise of only about 11 millibars in atmospheric pressure will lower the sea level by a tenth of a metre. A storm surge driving down the North Sea can raise tides by a metre or more above their predicted level. A generous safety margin is always required, therefore, not least because near real rocks or on a real bar, your boat will be bouncing up and down in the waves.

So in most situations at sea, the Rule of Twelfths applied with a bit of common sense and caution is going to be sufficient. It might even come in handy in the examination if you are running out of time on a complex navigational question. But a yachtmaster is expected to know the theory and be able to apply it when necessary. A complete assessment paper has been devoted to tides, treating the predictions as if they were exact, and you have to get the *Admiralty* method clear in your mind.

The notes accompanying the RYA's practice navigation tables therefore take great care to explain the full method for doing the two basic calculations that crop up in various forms – finding the predicted height of the tide at a given time, and finding when the tide will reach a certain height. They give examples using undated tables and curves you can use throughout the course.

To find the height of tide (at a standard port) at a given time between high and low water:

    (i) Look up the time of HW at the relevant port (remembering to convert from GMT to BST if necessary).

    (ii) Establish from that how many hours before or after HW your given time is.

    (iii) Look up the heights of HW and LW and subtract one from the other to give the range on that day.

    (iv) Apply the time difference before or after HW you established at (ii) to the tidal curves and note the equivalent factors for springs and neaps.

    (v) Compare the actual range with the ranges shown for springs and neaps, and if necessary interpolate between the two factors noted at (iv) to calculate one appropriate factor.

(vi) Multiply the range by the appropriate factor to give the height above LW.

(vii) Add the height above LW to the LW height to give the height of tide.

To find the time at which the tide will reach a given height (at a standard port):

(i) Look up the time of HW at the relevant port (and convert from GMT if necessary).

(ii) Look up the heights of HW and LW and subtract one from the other to give the range.

(iii) Subtract the LW height noted at (ii) from the given height of tide to establish the height above LW you require.

(iv) Divide the height above LW noted from (iii) by the range to find the factor they represent.

(v) Apply this factor to the tidal curves and note the equivalent intervals before or after HW (an examiner should make it clear which you need) for springs and neaps.

(vi) Compare the actual range with the ranges shown for springs and neaps, and if necessary interpolate between the two intervals noted at (v) to calculate one appropriate interval before or after HW.

(vii) Apply this interval to the time of HW to find the required time.

Unfortunately, the few dozen standard ports for which the times and heights of high and low water are quoted in the Admiralty tables are too far apart for accurate predictions at intermediate points along the coast. The tables therefore list secondary ports for each standard port, with time and height differences. Dover's secondary ports, for example, are Ramsgate, Deal, Folkestone, Dungeness, Rye and Hastings. In each case four time corrections are given, to add to or subtract from the times quoted for Dover, and four height corrections. The time corrections come in two pairs, for high and low water, distinguished by the time of day at which they should be applied – which is another way of saying they apply to either springs or neaps. The height corrections are specifically identified as being for springs or neaps. To find precisely the right corrections for a particular time and tide requires more interpolation. If the range of possible corrections is wide, it might help to draw a graph, but only the most meticulous of navigators could justify such an elaborate procedure for such a small gain in accuracy.

In *Reed's Nautical Almanac* the tidal predictions are laid out rather differently, and in a slightly condensed form. For example, the tidal

Oscar

differences between standard and secondary ports are only given as mean values, not distinguishing between springs and neaps. But the loss of such detail is compensated for by additional information, such as the 'guiding depth' at the entrance to the various harbours.

In the 1983 edition, *Reed's* have replaced the tables of tidal range and height by a rise of tide graph – that is a set of standard tidal curves – which is similar in concept to the *Admiralty* presentation. Additional low water predictions have also eliminated the characteristic *Reed's* arithmetic which involved subtracting the duration of mean rise and doubling the mean level. The relatively new *Macmillan and Silk Cut Nautical Almanac* closely follows the *Admiralty* method.

As we pointed out earlier, whenever tidal calculations are simplified, either to save space, as in an almanac, or to save time, as in the Rule of Twelfths, the potential error will be greater where the rise or fall is asymmetrical or the range is large. The practical seagoing message, therefore, is to adapt your method to the circumstances. Before crossing an exposed bar on a fast flowing ebb, it is obviously worth taking more trouble with your arithmetic, and allowing a bigger safety margin at the end, than when easing into a muddy estuary on the flood.

Perhaps the most common reason for using *Reed's* tide tables is simply that yachtsmen have the almanac on board anyway for the vast amount of other information it contains on everything from signals to seamanship. Almost any question in the Yachtmaster examinations which asks for the source of a particular piece of information can safely be answered by a reference to *Reed's*, which has long been regarded as a sort of yachtsman's bible, or since 1981 to *Macmillan's*.

Besides tides and tidal streams (which we discuss later), *Reed's* and *Macmillan* have sections on astro and coastal navigation, the collision regulations, port entry signals, radio aids, signalling, weather forecasting, safety and first aid, plus a comprehensive list of visual navigational aids and fog signals for UK and continental waters.

Tidal streams

Information on tidal streams comes in two main forms – special little chartlets covered in arrows and, on Admiralty charts, tidal diamonds marked at appropriate positions and referring to tables of direction and speed in the margin. In the Admiralty tidal stream atlases, in the almanacs, and on the sets of chartlets included on special yachting charts, the streams at each hour before and after high water at a given port are shown by a pattern of arrows marked with the speed in knots at springs and neaps. The direction of a tidal stream (that is, the direction in which it is flowing, not the direction from which it has come as with a wind) is known technically as the set; its rate in knots is the drift. The letter inside a tidal diamond refers to a table which gives both kinds of information, for springs and neaps, for the same hourly intervals before and after high water. A specially prepared tidal diamond table has in the past been included in the Yachtmaster course notes for use with the practice chart.

Practical points to remember about tidal streams are that they tend to set into bays, and be accelerated into tide rips or races where they have to force their way past headlands like Portland Bill or the Lizard, or squeeze through a bottleneck like the notorious Pentland Firth. On a spring ebb, even the sandy river bars of the east coast can easily produce standing waves that will fill a small boat's cockpit. A big race produces alarming, unpredictable waves even in calm weather and if it is blowing they should be avoided unless, as sometimes happens, there is a calm eddying patch close inshore through which you can slip.

Before moving on to the application of tidal stream calculations, and to chartwork in general, there are one or two other basic sources of which you should be aware.

The partial Admiralty equivalent of *Reed's* navigational aids is the *Admiralty List of Lights and Fog Signals*, which omits small navigational buoys. A point to remember here is that bearings of lights – for example to indicate the sector over which a light shows red or white – are recorded as they appear from the ship to seaward.

The Admiralty also publishes a long series of sailing directions or pilots, authoritative works of reference traditionally famous for their little sketches of 'conspic.' landmarks and grim warnings to navigators, but written for ships not yachts. The yachtsman is usually better served by the *Cruising Association Handbook*, which gives detailed pilotage information for approaching and berthing in a wide range of ports and harbours, from the perspective of a small vessel, or by one of the many still more detailed pilot books that cover a particular cruising area.

Chartwork

The essential instruments you need for chartwork are a ruler (the longest you can find, preferably made of transparent plastic), a parallel rule for transferring bearings from a compass rose to another part of the chart, a

Port-hand buoy

pair of dividers for measuring distance from the latitude scale (one minute of latitude equals a nautical mile), a pair of compasses for drawing arcs, a couple of soft hexagonal pencils (they will not roll so much) and a big soft rubber (the alternative combination of hard pencils and a small harsh rubber will soon destroy the surface on heavily used corners of the practice chart). One other simple instrument that is useful in the classroom and at sea on a small boat is a Douglas protractor – a square of transparent plastic with a hole in the centre and marked in degrees round the edges. This can be used to lay off compass bearings from the chart's grid, or as an alternative to a piece of tracing paper or a special device called a station pointer when fixing a central position from a sequence of bearings.

The symbols you should use as you come to them are:

△   estimated position

⊙   observed position (looks like an eye)

⊗*1500*   fix (position obtained from two or more position lines)

—→—   water track or wake course (relative to the water)

—↠—   ground track or course made good (relative to land)

—⇶—   tidal stream or current

——→   position line

←——↠   transferred position line

Nearly all the problems you will be asked to solve on the practice chart are variants of three basic geometrical calculations – fixing the yacht's present position, working out the course you should steer to reach a given position, and deciding where you have actually arrived after steering a given course for a certain time.

Obtaining a fix

The object of this exercise is to obtain two or more position lines. These are the lines along which the yacht's position must lie, so that if they intersect, and they are accurate, there is only one place she can be.

The most commonly used form of position line is a compass bearing of a visible object marked on the chart – a lighthouse, a buoy, or a tower described by the traditional chartmaker's abbreviation 'conspic.'. The nearer the object, incidentally, the less the bearing's inaccuracy will affect your position. Other forms of position line include the bearing of a radio beacon, the extended transit between two visible objects, the distance off a coastline, the dipping distance of a lighthouse, a line of soundings or even a single sounding if it establishes a position on a clearly defined seabed contour.

The classic application of a transit is a pair of leading marks or leading lights which, when kept in line, show the safest way into a harbour or the best water over a difficult bar. A transit (preferably between objects a good distance apart) can therefore be extremely useful just on its own. To take other examples of which the RYA examiners are fond: two objects can be chosen so that as long as one is kept 'open' of the other (that is they are not yet in transit) the yacht will stay clear of a dangerous area of shoals or rocks; or the appearance of a transit between them may be used as a kind of visual alarm clock, to remind the helmsman when to change course or go about from one tack to the other.

Depth soundings have always been used by seamen as a warning that they are 'standing into danger' (remember the letter U ··−). Indeed some modern echo sounders incorporate a depth alarm.

But when any of these methods is used to fix a single, specific position, you need at least two position lines, preferably at a fairly broad angle to one another. It's the principle you apply instinctively when sailing past, say, Walton pier − or Brighton pier if you are a south coast man − and you think: 'We're about two miles off, sailing roughly parallel with the shore, and the pier's abeam, so we must be about ... there on the chart.'

Position lines for a fix can be obtained from a compass bearing, a transit, a distance off, or a line of soundings.

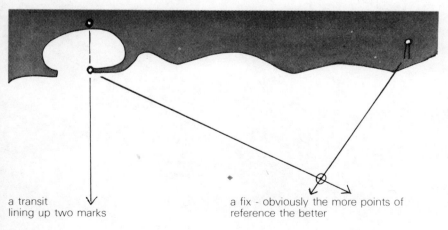

a transit
lining up two marks

a fix - obviously the more points of reference the better

Alpha

One way of improving on guesswork for the distance off is a dodge known as doubling the angle on the bow. Looking at the diagram you will see that if you take a bearing of an object on the shore and then maintain a steady course until the angle that bearing makes with your heading has doubled, the three relevant lines plotted on the chart form a triangle with two equal sides. If you have a log, you know the length of one of those sides – the distance the yacht has travelled – and that is also the distance off.

One combination of position lines big ships used before the days of radar, and which can still be useful aboard a yacht, is the bearing of a lighthouse at night and its dipping distance. Because of the curvature of the earth, distant objects eventually fall below the horizon. Using tables provided for this purpose in nautical almanacs, the distance at which a light of given height dips below the horizon can be found, and added to the extra visible distance

Doubling the angle on the bow. If a bearing is taken on a known point to find the angle it makes from the ship's bow (in this case 30°) and another taken when that figure is doubled (ie 60°), the distance between the two points from which the bearings were taken will be the same as the ship's distance from the known point.

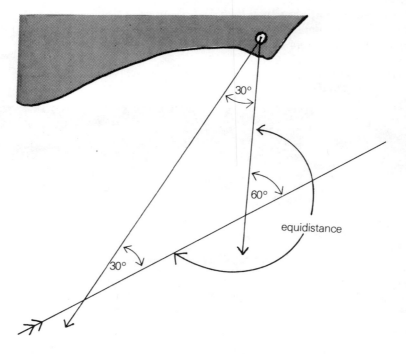

provided by the observer's own height above sea level. The position line produced in this way is a circle round the light whose radius is that total distance. A compass bearing intersecting the circle then gives a fix.

Two things to remember when doing this calculation:

(i) the charted height of a lighthouse is measured from high water springs, so if it's not HWS you have to add on the difference between that and the actual tidal level before consulting the distance table

(ii) be careful that the examiner does not try to catch you out by inviting you to use a light when the yacht is still beyond its luminous range

One general warning about bearings is to avoid taking them from objects like headlands and hills which may look clearcut from seaward, but whose precise location on a two dimensional chart is difficult to establish. Remember also that a back bearing from something you have passed may be just as useful as one taken from an object you are approaching – although in practice people often forget to look behind them.

If you take three bearings, they are far more likely to form a triangular 'cocked hat' on the chart than to meet at a single precise point. In that case you cannot guarantee that the yacht's position is inside the triangle, but it is more probably in the middle and you should assume that in plotting the fix.

Even if only a single identifiable object is visible it may still be possible to establish what is known as a running fix by taking two successive bearings. The first bearing is plotted and the log mileage at that time recorded. After a suitable interval a second bearing of the same object is taken and the course made good during the interval, allowing for the tidal stream, is plotted from any point on the first bearing or position line. This first line is then transferred, as in the diagram, so as to mark the only point on the second line where the track made good actually fits between the two bearings. That must be the yacht's position.

If only the angle between two identifiable objects can be measured – either by using a sextant horizontally, or from compass bearings whose deviation is constant but unknown – it will not fix the yacht's position but it will provide a position line in the form of a circle that also passes through the two objects. A second angle provides another circular position line and the intersection of the two circles gives a fix. More simply, the adjacent angles formed by a line of three identifiable objects can be measured and plotted, either on a piece of tracing paper, on the back of a Douglas protractor, or with the arms of a station pointer, and then manoeuvred over the chart until they fit. The yacht's position is fixed where the angles converge.

Juliet

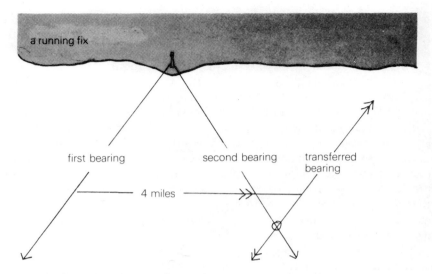

A running fix. Take a bearing from a known point and plot it on the chart. Then run a recorded distance (4 miles in this example) and take a second bearing. Transfer the first bearing 4 miles to intersect the second. Your fix is where the two position lines cross.

Plotting a course

Steer due north by your boat's compass and it is extremely unlikely that you will actually travel in a true northerly direction over the ground. To start with the compass is pointing not to true north, but to the magnetic pole (the variation we discussed earlier, see page 16), and it almost certainly has some additional deviation. If yours is a sailing boat with the wind ahead or on the beam, she will also be making leeway – that is, moving slightly crabwise, perhaps 5° downwind of the direction her bows are pointing. And she will also be affected by the tidal stream. This may simply help her along or cancel out some of her progress through the water (a boat motoring at 4½ knots with a 1½ knot tide under her travels twice as fast over the ground as the same boat heading into the tide – 6 knots instead of 3 – which is why it is so important for small craft to work their tides); but the stream sometimes sets across your course, altering hour by hour, and this has to be allowed for, along with the other factors mentioned above, when plotting the track, or course made good over the ground. The method is as illustrated in the diagram opposite.

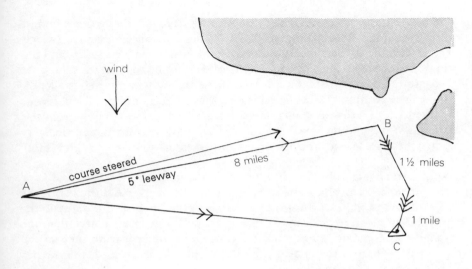

(i) add or subtract deviation to convert compass course (C) to magnetic (M)
(ii) subtract westerly variation to convert magnetic course (M) to true (T)
(iii) lay off the resulting true course steered from the fixed starting position A, and label it
(iv) apply leeway downwind (in this example 5°) and label the resulting wake course or water track
(v) measure the distance run through the water since leaving A against the adjacent latitude scale (in this example 8 miles in 2 hours) and mark it off along the wake course to give position B
(vi) look up the set and drift of the tidal stream during these same two hours and lay them off from B as two successive vectors of appropriate length and direction, one for each hour, so as to establish the estimated position C
(vii) connect A and C to give an approximation of the yacht's track, or course made good over the ground, and complete the velocity triangle

Estimated position

The accuracy of the estimated position will depend, among other things, on the accuracy of the helmsman's steering, the allowance for leeway (which varies with the type of boat and the set of the sails), the log reading and the tidal stream predictions. The process is often referred to as dead reckoning, because the position is deduced from these factors without independently fixing her position. (More specifically, a dead reckoning (DR) position, marked with a cross, is sometimes defined as one derived simply from the course steered and the distance run, without allowance for tides or leeway. When these are applied the position is known as an estimated position (EP).)

Shaping a course from one given position to another
In a sense this is just the same triangular problem in reverse, anticipating the effect of tide and leeway instead of working it out after the event. Again the method is illustrated in the diagram below. Note particularly that the yacht's progress along her track AB is not measured off from the starting point A, but from the end of the tidal vectors C, because this is often a source of misunderstanding:
  (i) lay off the desired track from A to B
  (ii) calculate roughly how long the trip will take (in this example something over two hours) and lay off the appropriate tidal vectors to point C

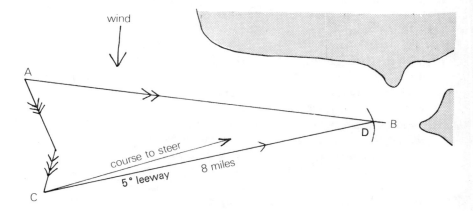

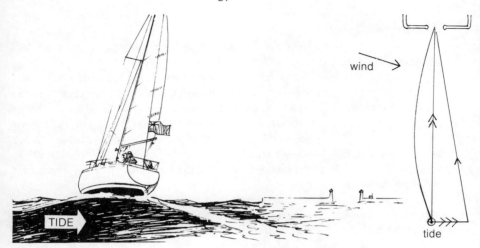

Much of the chart work in this section of the course would be a great deal simpler if there were no such things as tidal streams. These may carry your boat bodily sideways — as if on a moving carpet — and turn the straight line of your course into a potentially confusing triangle of velocities. In practice a sum of all the vectors can be plotted and the actual course may be a shallow curve. Charts and tidal atlases enable the navigator to shape a course and subsequently plot it to allow for tide.

(iii) with compasses set to the distance the yacht will cover during the same two hours, strike an arc from C through the desired track AB and mark it D, so that CD is the wake course required to reach the nearest practical point to B

(iv) compare the wake course with the magnetic compass rose and label it

(v) apply the appropriate corrections for leeway and deviation (both of which you will be given in the examination question) to obtain the compass course to steer

As you can see, this is a rather clumsy procedure which actually takes the yacht in a shallow curve from A to D. If it is necessary to stay close to the track between A and B each hour's tidal stream could be plotted to produce a separate course to steer. Alternatively, a succession of tidal vectors could be plotted to scale and then averaged to produce a single mean course to steer for the whole trip. As you near B, so you must plot your EP and adjust course to hit it off exactly.

Kilo

The ship's log

There are various reasons for keeping a log, or record, of your yacht's progress, and various types of log result.

The navigator may keep his own, with details of weather, tides and courses arranged to make his calculations easier. On larger vessels where the crew is formally organized into watches, a deck log is filled in as things occur, and at regular intervals. It thus provides at least the essential data for the navigator's DR plot – that is time, log reading and course. Other advantages are that the next watch know what has been happening while they were below. It could also be an important document in the event of a collision, for example.

As a minimum the course steered and distance logged must be entered every half an hour. The time intervals may not be exact but the actual time the log is read must be recorded. The log is also noted at the moment of any change of course (such as when tacking or gybing). From time to time the true wind force and direction and the barometer reading might also be recorded. On a motor yacht you might include engine information such as rpm, temperature, charging rate and fuel state.

METEOROLOGY

Apart from the sheer pleasure of understanding our daily weather, the study of meteorology is obviously valuable to the yachtsman.

On passage, he wants to recognize the first signs of an approaching depression, with its rain, gales and wind shifts. Racing inshore, he makes use of more local effects, like the summer sea breezes. In the classroom, preparing for his Yachtmaster's he also needs to know something of meteorological theory, with its special language, and in this context the practical aspect of the course is likely to be taking down a broadcast weather forecast and to draw his own weather map from it – as part of the meteorology assessment paper.

Fortunately, much of the weathermen's technical jargon is already familiar from newspaper forecast maps, and above all from radio and television. We are used to looking at patterns of 'isobars', and hearing about 'advancing depressions' and 'associated troughs'. We even see satellite pictures of the swirling clouds that mark their progress.

The meteorology section of the RYA course is a matter of going back to first principles and working through them coherently, learning the definitions as you go along. You then have to put in the practice necessary to draw a passable map of your own – not a difficult thing if you have unlimited time, but quite a feat within the short sketching time allowed by an examination.

The basic weather system

The most basic distinction we generally draw when describing the weather is between a warm day and a cold one. And in truth, temperature ultimately determines the other characteristics that interest us – whether it is wet or dry, sunny or cloudy, windy or calm.

In North West Europe, we live roughly on the boundary of the cold air masses of the Polar regions and the warm air of the Tropics. The line where they meet is known as the polar front.

Foxtrot

The density of air varies with its temperature, so a warm pocket of air tends to float to the top of the surrounding cooler mass, just as a cold pocket of air descends. The movement – sometimes a complete circulation – set up by the tendency of warmer air to rise, is known as convection. As the air rises it cools, one way in which the invisible water vapour carried by any air, but especially warm air, which can carry more of it, condenses into visible droplets of cloud or fog. Convective cumulus cloud, the fluffy white kind of a child's picture book, is the result of this process, and any other cooling process will have a similar effect, although the visual result may be quite different.

In other words, the amount of water vapour air can absorb before it becomes saturated increases with temperature. As cooling air reaches this varying point of saturation, it is said to be at the dew point. If it gets any cooler the excess water vapour will condense.

The warm moist air inside your car mists over the inside of a cold windscreen because the glass cools it below its dew point. More relevantly, warm moist air advancing from subtropical regions across colder northern seas – from the Azores into the Western Approaches, for example – will tend to release its excess moisture as fog. It consists of water droplets, just like the convective cloud, but we give it a different name because the air from which it condenses is cooler than the mass above it. There is no convective tendency to rise, so the fog characteristically drifts near the surface.

In general, a mixed air mass with the cooler, denser air at the bottom, is going to be stable. One with warmer, less dense air temporarily trapped at its base will be unstable – a characteristic of Polar air masses moving south over warmer seas. The Polar front, along which moving air masses of different temperatures tend to meet and swirl, is also likely to be an area of complex instability.

A depression, the most prominent single feature of the weather along the coastlines of North West Europe, often starts as no more than a ripple on the Polar front way out in the Atlantic. A bulge of warm subtropical air pushes into and over a cooler northern air mass and begins to swirl upwards. The bulge becomes a moving wave, with a warm front on its leading edge and a cold front on its trailing edge as the cooler air closes in behind it. And if, as often happens, the cold front eventually overtakes the warm front, cutting off its supply of warm air, the fronts are said to be occluded (compare occulting lights).

The depression, centred on the crest of the wave, is therefore an area of

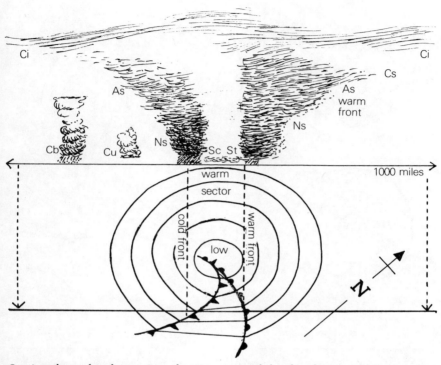

Section through a depression, showing types of cloud and areas of rain. Most depressions are more complex than this, but the basic features can usually be recognized.

ascending air and low pressure, by comparison with the surrounding areas of relatively high pressure, where cool air is either gently descending or at least stable. Pressure can be measured with a barometer – on yachts it's usually the compact aneroid kind – and shown on a scale divided into millibars. The pressures we are concerned with fluctuate around the 1000 millibar level, with less than 940 millibars in a really deep 'low', and more than 1040 millibars in an intense 'high', ie a 100 millibar range. A complete area of high pressure is known as an anticyclone (the opposite word, cyclone, being reserved for vigorous Tropical depressions) and a ridge of high pressure may be said to be dividing two lows. Within a depression, pressure is especially low along the line of the two fronts, which are therefore important examples of what is known as a trough.

Bravo

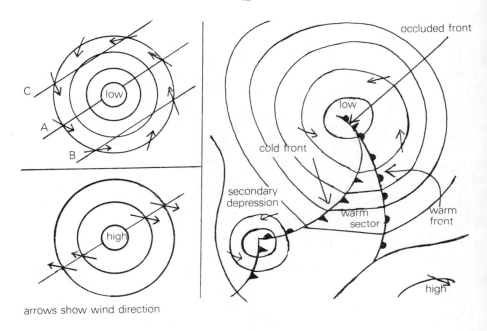

arrows show wind direction

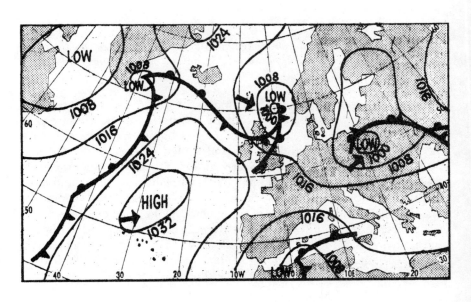

Meteorologists illustrate and analyse these features by drawing maps, or synoptic charts, covered in isobars – that is, lines of equal barometric pressure. The effect is to show the contours of a depression or anticyclone, just as height contours on a land map show the shape of a range of hills. On a weather map they also show the direction of the wind, because in the northern hemisphere air circulates anti-clockwise round a depression, along the contours but slightly inwards towards the centre, while round an anticyclone it circulates in the opposite direction, clockwise, and slightly outwards.

The contours of a depression tend to be steeper than those of an anticyclone, especially near its centre, and this shows up on the map in the closer spacing of the isobars. The winds are correspondingly stronger, often up to gale force and beyond, which is of course why yachtsmen should be on their guard against the approach of a deep low. In any case the rain and drizzle which usually accompany its passing fronts put it in the general category of bad weather, whereas a stationary anticyclone is often the source of a fine spell of summer weather.

Not all depressions come in from the Atlantic. For example in hot summer weather a thundery low sometimes forms in France and spreads across the Channel to bring its clouds into southern England. But the classic pattern of British weather – and certainly the one most relevant to passing the Yachtmaster's meteorology examination – is caused by a depression tracking north east across the British Isles until it disappears somewhere over the Baltic. The clouds that signal its approach, the falling barometer, the wind shifts marking its contours – these are the raw material of all those old weather sayings about mackerel skies, the moon hiding her head in a halo and winds that shift against the sun.

Look at an isobaric chart of a symmetrical low, and you will see that if it passes directly overhead, moving north east, the wind will shift through 180° after a brief lull – roughly from south east to north west. On our diagram, the observer's viewpoint moves along track A.

If the centre of low pressure passes to the north, a southerly wind will veer – that is, shift in a clockwise direction – until it becomes westerly (track B). If the low passes to the south the wind will back – anticlockwise – from an

Top left: The basic wind patterns of 'low' and 'high' in the northern hemisphere. Right: Additional features in practice – fronts, and a secondary. Bottom: How the weather systems appear on a chart in a newspaper, on one day in the year.

Ground track

easterly to a northerly direction (track C). The barometer will fall and rise during the same period.

If you draw the chart a little more realistically to show the deeper troughs of low pressure accompanying the advancing warm and cold fronts, the wind shifts will be sharper at these points, especially at the passage of the cold front. And if this primary low has a secondary one developing on the tail of the cold front – quite likely more violent than its parent – the wind may back sharply only to veer again:

> When the wind shifts against the sun,
> Trust it not for back 'twill run.

Patterns of falling and rising pressure can be traced in the same way:

> When rise commences after low,
> Squalls expect and then clear blow.

Just as these patterns are the raw material of the old sayings, so the raw material of your weather map is the sequence of wind directions and speeds given in the BBC shipping forecast plus similar information, including the important barometric pressure readings, reported from the coastal weather stations. Join the points of equal pressure and by definition you have a few isobars to form the basis of your sketch map – though do not expect them to look so neat and obvious as the stylized diagrams in a textbook. Taken from a real shipping forecast, they can be maddeningly ambiguous.

Fortunately, the forecast also contains two other sorts of information: a general synopsis, which tells you where the main lows and highs are heading, and more conventional remarks such as whether it is raining in sea area Fastnet and how many miles they can see from the deck of the Noord Hinder light vessel. If you know from the synopsis that you are dealing with a low pressure system of a certain depth and movement, the coastal readings may give an idea of its shape. They are certainly indisputable elements of the picture. But if there is an obvious front moving across the British Isles, the reported wind directions, and the distribution of rain and poor visibility, may provide better clues.

Out at sea, the first sign of an approaching depression may be none of these, but rather the wispy 'mares' tails' driven far ahead of it by strong, high altitude winds:

> Mackerel sky and mares' tails,
> Make tall ships carry small sails.

Clouds
Meteorologists distinguish clouds according to their height and form, using

the Latin words *cumulus* (heap), *stratus* (blanket), and *cirrus* (curl of hair), to describe heaped up, layered and high wispy cloud respectively. The word *alto* may be added to indicate a medium level cloud of some particular form, and *nimbus* (storm cloud) means rain bearing. But the resulting classification is not totally logical and the main types simply have to be learned:

Cumulus (Cu)   low, mainly white, clouds piled into small heaps and usually associated with fine weather

Stratocumulus (Sc)   low heaped clouds gathered into an extensive layer

Cumulonimbus (Cb)   towering heaps of cloud that produce showers or thunderstorms

Stratus (St)   a low layer of featureless grey cloud

Nimbostratus (Ns)   layers of dark rain bearing cloud

Altocumulus (Ac)   medium level heaped clouds, in rounded, lens shaped or castellated form

Altostratus (As)   a medium level layer of cloud through which a 'watery' sun may be seen

Cirrus (Ci)   high level streaks of cloud formed by ice crystals, often referred to as 'mares' tails'

Cirrocumulus (Cc)   high level heaped clouds which may assume the regular rippled pattern – usually benign – of the 'mackerel sky'

Cirrostratus (Cs)   high level layered cloud which may produce a 'halo' round the sun or moon

Clouds are generally confined to the troposphere, the first 45,000 feet or so of the earth's atmosphere within which the temperature falls as you go higher. The troposphere ends at the tropopause, above which the temperature remains more or less constant with height. Just below the tropopause, strong jet stream winds of 100 mph or more often blow in the direction a depression is moving, carrying the high level clouds associated with it far ahead of the lower, heavier clouds which bring the rain. Cirrus clouds, therefore, are often a sign of approaching bad weather:

> If clouds look as if scratched by a hen,
> Get ready to reef your topsails then.

They are formed by showers of tiny ice crystals, falling through the strong upper winds and appearing to trail in one direction or another as their lateral movement slows down. The white streaks (either the tips or the roots of the 'mares' tails' according to which way round you visualize them) therefore point back towards the centre of low pressure advancing behind them. They also enable you to apply what is known as the crossed wind rule

Tango

– stand with your back to the surface wind and if the clouds show that the upper wind is coming from your left, the weather is probably deteriorating.

Two other types of cloud notably characteristic of a passing frontal depression are cirrostratus, the layered ice crystals that often produce a warning halo effect round the sun or moon as a clear sky clouds over, and cumulonimbus, the tall clouds that produce heavy rain showers as the unstable, blustery cold front comes through. But then by the time a complete low pressure system has come and gone, nearly all the cloud types may have been represented.

Cross section of a depression
A large depression may easily be 1000 miles in extent, with cloud stretching 500 miles ahead of the warm front. Its speed of movement may be anything up to about 60 knots – one of the hazards of weather forecasting – but on this scale you can see that it can take all day for the first warning cloud signs to be translated into the rain and turbulence of the frontal areas. Not that every depression produces rain. But assuming a vigorous low, with two distinct frontal troughs in the classic form, then the belt of rain along the warm front may be about 100 miles wide, and the cold front's rain belt perhaps 50 miles wide.

There are two useful ways of visualizing a depression:
 (i) looking down on the isobars of the familiar synoptic chart and imagining two big swirls of cloud accompanying the fronts, as seen sometimes quite clearly on the satellite pictures
 (ii) taking a vertical cross-section, which is most usefully drawn (as in our illustration) along a SW-NE axis that cuts across the two fronts

Now imagine the whole system tracking north east. The chart on page 42 (top right) shows the shifting wind directions as felt by a more or less stationary yacht on the surface, the likely strength of the wind, and the rise and fall of the barometer. The cross-section shows the advancing warm front with the succession of cloud formations that precede it, the warm sector, and the wedge of cold air closing in from behind it.

As the depression approaches the wind will back southerly and the classic progression of clouds will probably appear: high wispy streaks (of cirrus) spreading to shroud the sun (cirrostratus) and then steadily lowering and darkening (altostratus and nimbostratus) until the rain begins to fall – light at first, but soon settling into a continuous moderately heavy spell as the warm sector arrives. Meanwhile the wind will have increased. Visibility will remain good except through the rain.

Entering the warm sector, fog or drizzle may reduce visibility even though the rain has eased. The temperature will rise, although the generally damp conditions will probably disguise this. The most significant effect for yachtsmen may well be the veering wind, which should then stay steady until the arrival of the cold front, when it will veer again towards the north west, usually more sharply. The barometer will reflect the same basic pattern – steady, then rising rapidly.

If the low is a vigorous one, with steep pressure gradients and correspondingly strong winds (a fall in pressure of 5 or 6 millibars in 3 hours is considered 'rapid'), this is when they will be felt. The cold front is not only likely to bring heavy rain squalls; its generally gusty winds will accentuate the cooler, fresher atmosphere. Towering thundery clouds may even produce some hail. But at least the cold front tends to pass more quickly than its warm counterpart. To some extent the cloud sequence may be reversed, but the more important effect is the brisk procession of heaped up medium level clouds (cumulus or cumulonimbus) with clear blue sky soon to be seen above them. On land it's a cheerful moment – the arrival of the 'showers and bright periods' after a spell of miserable wet weather. At sea, it may mean pulling down the last reef and weathering the worst of the blow.

The anticyclone
For sailors, as for landsmen, high pressure generally means fine weather. The pressure gradients round an anticyclone are usually less steep than in a depression, so light winds are the rule and gales a rarity. While the air continues to descend in the area of high pressure, diverging outwards to feed the inward circulation of any neighbouring depressions, it is compressed, warmed and dried. Moisture picked up from the sea may condense out, but the incipient cloud is often stifled at low level by a temperature inversion – that is, a layer of warm air sitting on top of the cooler surface air in which the cloud starts to form. Anticyclonic weather may therefore be dull and foggy, but it seldom rains.

Local weather
With only moderate winds and sometimes clear skies, a slow moving anticyclone obviously gives more scope than a violent depression to local weather phenomena that may be just as important to the yachtsman during the few hours he is at sea than the large systems we have looked at so far. The first boat to pick up a sea breeze on the way home, for example, may win the club handicap race by half a mile.

Rock awash

Sea breezes are caused along the coast in summer when rising air above the rapidly heated land surface sucks in air from offshore. They are naturally confined to within a few miles of the coast and they do not rise above Force 3 or 4 on the Beaufort scale. A line of convective cumulus clouds over the coastline is a likely sign that a sea breeze is there to be used.

At night, when the land cools more rapidly than the sea, whose temperature scarcely changes, the reverse process may produce a land breeze, but it tends to be a weak affair by comparison. The daily pattern of temperatures, reaching their peak in mid-afternoon and their minimum soon after dawn, is known technically as the diurnal variation.

Where convection is more violent, round the base of a towering thundercloud, for example, the thermal up-draught can cause sudden squalls and localized wind shifts. The opposite sort of instability, when cold air rolls down the sides of a coastal valley or fjord, accentuating the night-time tendency to a land breeze, is called a katabatic wind.

For the racing yachtsman, the smallest of local effects – updraughts, downdraughts, wind shadows, eddies in the lee of a headland and so on – are worth anticipating. The cruising man, on the other hand, can pay too much attention to general weather forecasts, which never claim to be accurate to within a few miles or a few hours. Apart from the necessarily somewhat pedantic requirements of an examination, he only needs to be on the lookout for a few real dangers – a sudden deep low is one of them; fog in a crowded shipping lane another.

Fog
There are various forms of fog (including frontal fog, that develops where warm and cold air mix), but the two main types are radiation or land fog, and advection or sea fog.

The basic cause of fog, as explained earlier, is cooling air to the critical temperature, or dew point, below which it can no longer hold its moisture as invisible vapour. Surplus moisture then condenses out as water droplets suspended in the air.

Land fog occurs, generally in autumn and winter, when any warmth in the land is rapidly radiated into a clear sky and the air immediately above the surface is then cooled below its dew point. A light breeze may help to diffuse the cooling effect and spread the fog. Its importance to yachtsmen is that it may drift out to sea for a few miles, particularly at dawn, when it is most prevalent.

Sea fog may also arrive from landward in the sense that warm air heated, for example, over the European continent, may release fog when it starts to move across the cool water of the North Sea. Fog in the Channel, especially in spring and early summer, may be brought by a warm, moist, south westerly air stream blowing from the Azores across progressively colder seas. It is the critical relationship of temperatures and humidity that matters and unfortunately for seamen, once the potential for fog exists, a rising wind may not blow it away. Sea fog can persist in Force 5 or even 6.

The yachtsman who is also an amateur meteorologist may want to try his hand at forecasting sea fog, by taking the temperature of buckets full of sea water and measuring the dew point of the air with a whirling psychrometer (two thermometers, one of which has its bulb surrounded by a damp wick from which water is evaporating). For the rest of us, it's a matter of watching for a general tendency to fog, checking the local forecast, perhaps plotting a position more frequently, and trying not to get caught out in an awkward spot if it suddenly clamps down.

The Beaufort wind scale

Admiral Francis Beaufort's Scale of Wind Forces was originally defined in terms of the amount of sail a square rigged naval frigate could carry. Then it was fishing smacks. Now the scale is used on land and sea, with various ways of describing the effect of specified wind speeds. With experience, sailors relate the wind force they know is blowing on a given day to the effect it has on the boat or boats they are familiar with. Left to make their own assessment, most people tend at first to exaggerate, but then the written descriptions are not much help. We have included the effects seen on land, in case you find some useful point of reference there, perhaps while driving down to the boat and listening to the forecast on the car radio.

Force	Wind speed in knots	Forecast description	Wave height in metres	Sea state	Effects on land
0	Less than 1	Calm	0	Like a mirror	Smoke rises vertically
1	1-3	Light	0	Ripples without crests	Smoke, but not vanes, indicate wind direction
2	4-6	Light	0.1	Small wavelets, but crests do not break	Leaves rustle; wind vanes move
3	7-10	Light	0.4	Large wavelets; crests begin to break	Wind extends light flag
4	11-16	Moderate	1	Small waves; fairly frequent white horses	Wind raises dust and loose paper; small branches move

Echo

Single-letter signals

A I have a diver down; keep well clear at slow speed

B I am taking in, or discharging, or carrying dangerous goods

C Yes (affirmative or 'The significance of the previous group should be read in the affirmative')

D Keep clear of me; I am manoeuvring with difficulty

E I am altering my course to starboard

F I am disabled; communicate with me

G I require a pilot (when made by fishing vessels operating in close proximity on the fishing grounds it means 'I am hauling nets')

H I have a pilot on board

I I am altering my course to port

J I am on fire and have dangerous cargo on board; keep well clear of me

K I wish to communicate with you

L You should stop your vessel instantly

M My vessel is stopped and making no way through the water

N No (negative or 'The significance of the previous group should be read in the negative'). This signal may be given only visually or by sound. For voice or radio transmission the signal should be 'No'

O Man overboard

P In harbour: All persons should report on board as the vessel is about to proceed to sea

At sea: May be used by fishing vessels to mean 'My nets have come fast upon an obstruction'

Q My vessel is healthy and I request free pratique

S I am operating astern propulsion

T Keep clear of me; I am engaged in pair trawling

U You are running into danger

V I require assistance

W I require medical assistance

X Stop carrying out your intentions and watch for my signals

Y I am dragging my anchor

Z I require a tug (when made by fishing vessels operating in close proximity on the fishing grounds it means 'I am shooting nets')

We have tried to cut down on the number of lights illustrated in this section (and so make them easier to remember) by relying on your commonsense. This will tell you that if a drawing is captioned 'not under way' the addition of steaming lights would represent the same vessel making way. Similarly, all-round lights are shown by one drawing rather than three marked bow, stern and side; the single masthead light on a vessel under 50m would become two on a vessel over 50m long.

Plate 1

Morse Code, the International Code of Signals and reminders of their joint meanings. For full translation of each signal see opposite page.

Plate 2

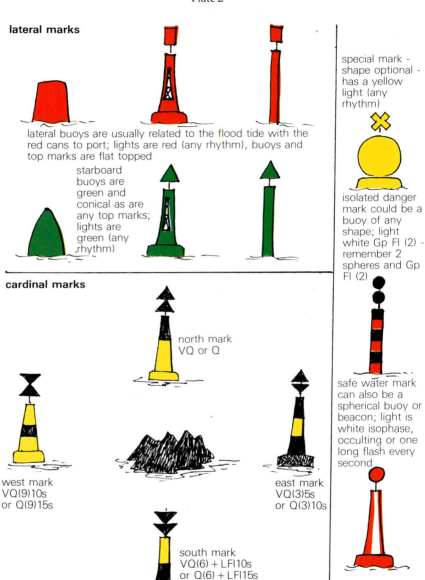

Plate 3

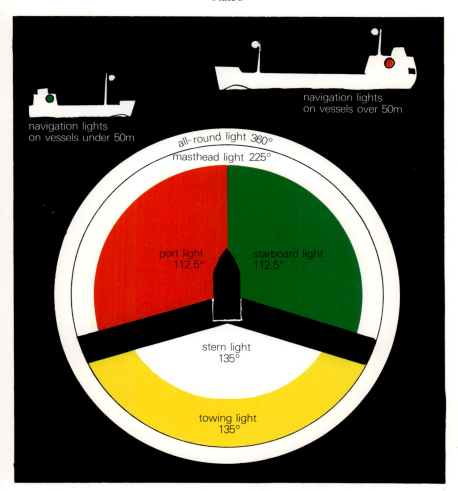

An easy way to remember the arcs of the navigation lights is that the stern light covers an arc made up of the first three odd numbers – 1,3,5 – 135°. Subtract this from 360° and you have the arc of the masthead light – 225°. Halve this and you have the arcs of the port and starboard lights – 112.5°. The all-round light is 360°.

Plate 4

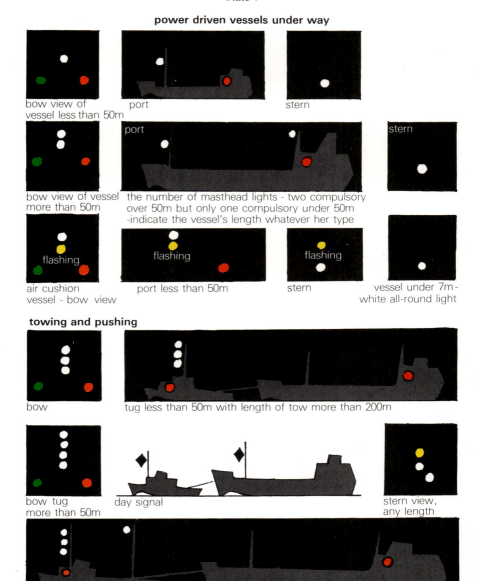

Plate 5

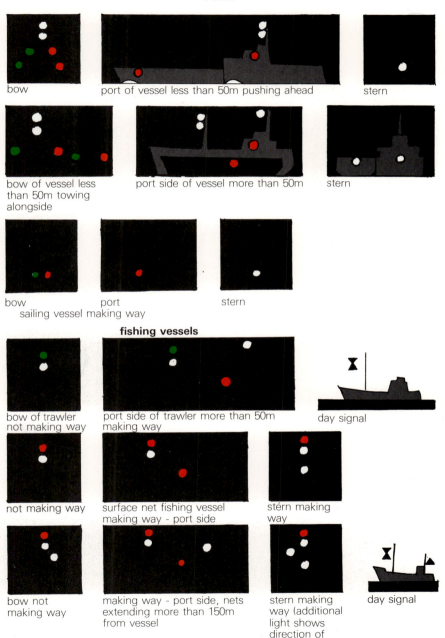

Plate 6

vessels not under command or restricted in their ability to manoeuvre

bow view - not under command

day signal (balls up?)

port side - not under command but making way

bow - vessel restricted in ability to manoeuvre

port side and making way

stern and making way

day signal (think of the diamond as the vessel that is restricted)

bow - anchored vessel restricted in her ability to manoeuvre

port side - more than 50m

day signal

bow - vessel less than 50m, towing and unable to deviate from her course

port (same red, white, red as above)

stern

mine sweepers

day signals

day signal

bow making way

dredgers

bow not making way

(double red lights indicate obstructed side)

day signal

when the size of the vessel prevents these shapes being shown a vessel engaged in underwater operations should fly the code flag A

Plate 7

vessels constrained by their draught

bow

more than 50m - port side

stern

day signal

pilot vessels

bow - at anchor

at anchor - less than 50m - port side

stern – making way

more than 50m

day signal - the red and white of the all-round lights are duplicated in the day signal

anchored vessels and vessels aground

at anchor - more than 50m - port side

day signal

bow

aground - less than 50m

stern

day signal

aground - more than 50m
(note preponderance of port red lights)

seaplanes

bow
port side

stern

Plate 8

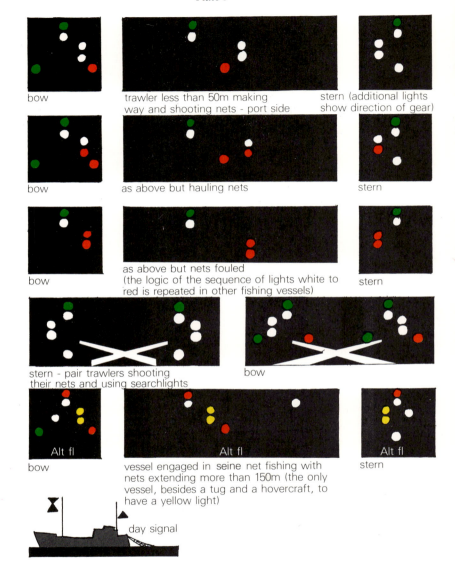

5	17-21	Fresh	2	Moderate, longer waves; many white horses	Small trees in leaf begin to sway
6	22-27	Strong breeze	3	Large waves with foam crests; spray likely	Telegraph wires whistle; umbrellas difficult to use
7	28-33	Near gale	4	Foam streaks begin to appear	Whole trees in motion
8	34-40	Gale	5.5	Longer waves, well marked with foam streaks	Twigs break off; walking difficult
9	41-47	Severe gale	7	High waves with dense streaks of foam, spray and tumbling crests	Slight structural damage, eg to chimney pots and slates
10	48-55	Storm	9	Very high waves with long overhanging crests and large patches of foam; tumbling crests are heavy; visibility is affected	Trees uprooted; considerable structural damage

Sources of weather information

Most weather forecasts originate from the Central Forecast Office of the Meteorological Office at Bracknell. They are broadcast by BBC Radio, by the various television channels, by local commercial radio stations, by the coastal radio stations, and through the automatic telephone weather service. Some newspapers also publish extensive forecasts.

All these sources are useful in their different ways. The tape recorded telephone forecasts for coastal areas are a convenient check before setting out on a trip, though they will probably yield less relevant information than a call to one of the local meteorological offices, some of which are open 24 hours a day. Television forecasts are not aimed at yachtsmen and are unlikely to be available on board your boat, but they do enable you to visualize the general pattern and movement of the weather. Some daily newspaper forecasts, though inevitably based on yesterday's information, have the considerable advantage of including a synoptic chart that can be kept for reference. But by far the most important source for yachtsmen, and the one which features largely in the Yachtmaster course, is the BBC shipping forecast, supported by detailed forecasts for inshore waters and the general regional forecasts which make a useful point of discussing the outlook for the next couple of days. Coastal radio stations also broadcast that section of the shipping forecast which covers their area – at different times from the BBC, which is helpful, and updated as necessary.

wind force 0

force 3, average 9 knots
probable wave height 2 feet

force 5, average 18 knots
probable wave height 6 feet

force 8, average 37 knots
probable wave height 18 feet

sail carried by an average
20-footer in varying conditions

The shipping forecast

This is broadcast on Radio 4 (1500 metres or 200 kHz) four times a day at 0015, 0625, 1355 and 1750. It includes a summary of gale warnings (which are also broadcast after news bulletins or at other convenient moments, and are visually conveyed by hoisting north or south cones, reminiscent of the cardinal buoyage topmarks, at certain coastal vantage points), a general synopsis, individual forecasts for sea areas round the British Isles, and reports from coastal stations.

The synopsis gives the position of the main depressions, anticyclones, troughs and fronts on the latest chart analysed at the Central Forecast Office (that is about 6 hours previously), the central pressure of the lows and highs, and their expected movement over the following 24 hours.

The sea area forecasts come next, always in the same order, starting with Viking, off Norway, and going round the British Isles in clockwise fashion to finish in South East Iceland. Details are given of wind, weather and visibility for the following 24 hours.

The 5-minute bulletin ends with the reports from coastal stations, a similar clockwise sequence – Tiree, Sumburgh, Bell Rock lighthouse, Dowsing light vessel, Noord Hinder light vessel, Varne light vessel, Royal Sovereign light tower, Channel light vessel, Scilly, Valentia, Ronaldsway and Malin lighthouses – describing the wind direction and force, the weather (rain, snow, showers etc), the visibility in miles or yards, the pressure in millibars (mb) and how it is changing.

Regional inshore waters forecasts are broadcast twice a day, covering up to 12 miles offshore. In the morning they are broadcast on Radio 3 (247 metres or 1214 kHz) at 0655 on weekdays and 0755 at weekends. At night they normally follow the midnight shipping forecast on Radio 4 (1500 metres or 200 kHz), Radio Scotland (810 kHz) and Radio Ulster (1341 kHz). Their purpose is to give more detail of local, coastal, weather conditions.

The language of these forecasts is precise and economical. Superfluous words like 'wind force' and 'visibility' are omitted, while those that are used each have a careful definition. The definitions should be learned both to

The Beaufort scale was originally based on the characteristics of a nineteenth century frigate at sea. Later it was adapted for yachtsmen and based on the sail carried by fishing smacks. Nowadays the variety of sailing craft is such that every skipper must make his own decision in relation to what his craft will stand; the trend is to think of the wind speed in knots.

India

understand them and because they may be the subject of specific questions in the meteorology assessment paper.

Warnings of 'gales' are issued if mean wind speeds of Force 8 (34-40 knots) or gusts of more than 48 knots are expected within the following 24 hours or might occur within the next 12 hours. 'Severe gales' indicate a mean wind speed of Force 9 (41-47 knots) or gusts of more than 51 knots; 'storm' means Force 10 (48-55 knots) or gusts of more than 60 knots.

If a gale is 'imminent', it should arrive within 6 hours of the warning being issued; 'soon' means within 6 to 12 hours; 'later' means more than 12 hours away.

'Pressure systems' are said to move either:
    slowly – up to 15 knots
    steadily – 15 to 25 knots
    rather quickly – 25 to 35 knots
    rapidly – 35 to 45 knots
    very rapidly – over 45 knots (ie the basic interval is 10 knots)

'Visibility' in the sea area forecasts is defined as:
    good – more than 5 nautical miles
    moderate – 2 to 5 miles
    poor – 1100 yards to 2 miles
    fog – less than 1100 yards

The 'pressure tendency' is described in terms of what it has been doing within the past 3 hours:
    steady – less than 0.1 millibar change
    rising or falling slowly – 0.1 to 1.5 millibar change
    rising or falling – 1.6 to 3.5 millibars
    rising or falling quickly – 3.6 to 6.0 millibars
    rising or falling very rapidly – more than 6.0 millibars
    now falling or now rising – change from rising to falling or vice versa

To take down all this information and plot it on your own weather map, you need pads of printed forms and maps of the kind published by the RYA and the Meteorological Office especially for yachtsmen. The forms are laid out to match the sequence of the shipping forecast and the maps show the British Isles with the various sea areas and coastal stations marked in. They may also have a set of geostrophic scales with which you can convert the spacing of the isobars into Beaufort wind forces or knots, according to whether you are measuring along a warm front or a cold front – when the wind speed for a given spacing will be somewhat higher. The rule is that a pressure gradient of 1 millibar in 30 nautical miles gives a surface wind of about 24 knots (Force 6).

It would be impossible to get down all the information contained in the shipping forecast without using some form of abbreviation or shorthand, however informal. Meteorologists have their own international plotting symbols to describe the weather, and there is also a Beaufort notation, using single letters which apart from p for showers are what you might expect.

Weather	Beaufort notation	Plotting symbol
Rain	r	●
Drizzle	d	❟
Snow	s	✳
Showers	p	▽
Hail	h	△
Thunder	t	↖
Squalls	q	∀
Mist	m	=
Fog	f	≡
Haze	z	∞
Calm	o	⊙

Beaufort wind forces are shown by little half feathered arrows pointing in the direction the wind is blowing. A southerly Force 1 would be shown ⌐ , a northerly Force 3 ⌐ , and a westerly gale Force 8 ⌐ .

Although the symbols make for a more professional looking map, most students seem to prefer the letters and numbers for taking down the forecast because they are easier to learn and just as quick to write. Other useful symbols are a horizontal arrow to show that something – perhaps a wind direction and force – is 'becoming' something else, and an oblique line to indicate the forecaster's habitual distinction between the situation 'at first' and 'later'.

The coastal reports are easier to take down than the sea area forecasts because the pattern of information is clearly fixed. In the last column, recording the pressure tendency or change, it's a simple dodge to use a horizontal line to mean 'steady', a gently sloping one to mean 'falling slowly' or 'rising slowly', and so on. 'Falling more slowly' becomes a kinked line that slopes down and then horizontally; 'now rising' is a V shape. The

Safe water mark

instructor is bound to have his own tips and then it's a question of working out your own personal shorthand and practising it as often as possible, using tape recordings of actual forecasts, for instance. Note, incidentally, that the synopsis and the coastal reports are for different times.

In the examination, where the object of the exercise has been to draw a convincing synoptic chart, it is vital to concentrate on getting the general synopsis down, even if you miss out some of the sea area forecasts because they are read too fast. Lows and highs can be noted down just with the capital letter L or H and the last two numbers of the pressure readings. In the same way there is no need to specify miles or yards when recording the visibility, because it will be obvious. If you get behind with the coastal reports, which is less likely than with the sea areas, give priority to the pressures, because these should help you draw in the first few isobars. Then let your imagination loose to create the basic picture on which you can embroider the local weather pattern.

SAFETY AND SEAGOING PRACTICE

The rule of the road

You need not be a sailor to know that ships carry a green navigation light on their starboard side and a red one to port, or that steam traditionally gives way to sail. Hire a motor cruiser on the Thames and the boatman will probably explain that in a narrow channel it is customary to 'drive on the right'.

Such basic principles were evolved as part of what maritime lawyers call 'the ordinary practice of seamen'. But nowadays they are codified, along with many much more complex rules, in the International Regulations for Preventing Collisions at Sea – the collision regulations, for short.

The current regulations date from 1972 and they came into force in 1977. They were drafted by a branch of the United Nations known as the International Maritime Organisation – IMO (formerly IMCO). The Organisation has its headquarters in London and its members, more than a hundred of them, include all the major maritime flag states.

The 1972 regulations superseded those drafted in 1960. The main changes took account of the widespread introduction of radar (in an effort to prevent further 'radar assisted collisions'), the special needs of giant tankers that might be 'constrained by their draught', and the new concept of traffic separation schemes. The need for this last provision, a system of one-way shipping lanes through congested waters, or maritime dual carriageways, had been fatally emphasized the previous year by a series of casualties in the Dover Strait.

The new regulations also modified and updated the rules governing the behaviour of sailing vessels. The fundamental principle of steam giving way to sail survived, but only just. It was severely constrained by other rules effectively giving priority to large commercial craft.

The regulations come in four parts:

A – general rules and definitions
B – steering and sailing rules
C – lights and shapes
D – sound and light signals

Vessel restricted in ability to manoeuvre

They are nearly all of great practical importance at sea, whether you are commanding a 5-ton yacht or a 50,000-ton tanker, and they form a correspondingly large part of the Yachtmaster Offshore syllabus whether in the classroom or at sea. We have therefore presented them virtually complete, but with accompanying notes to give some perspective, and using different type faces to distinguish sections of the text. There is not much more we can do to make them digestible except to point out that there is a practical seagoing logic to be found deep in the legal jargon – as in the basic principle that small vessels with freedom to manoeuvre give way to larger ones restricted by their size and draught. In other words although lawyers drafted the regulations, seamen told them what to write.

The text set in italic denotes rules that are of direct or special relevance to yachtsmen. The steering rules for sailing vessels obviously come into this category – starboard tack has right of way, and so on – as do the navigation lights that must be carried by different types of yacht.

The text in capitals indicates key phrases, or in some cases complete regulations, that may be worth learning by heart the day before the examination or glancing through just before it starts. Some of these are simply definitions, some are revision checklists, others are important because they convey in carefully drafted legal language some rule or principle that might otherwise be difficult to convey without ambiguity. The obligations of the 'stand-on vessel' in a crossing situation are a good example. Another, of great significance to yachtsmen because they have been heavily fined for disregarding it, is a rule stating that vessels crossing traffic separation lines shall do so 'as nearly as practicable at right angles to the general direction of traffic flow'.

International regulations for preventing collisions at sea, 1972
Part A – General rules and definitions
[Examiners sometimes show a surprising predilection for broad questions of definition, or tricky ones of the 'When is a door not a door?' variety. For that reason, this first section of the rules is worth more attention than you might otherwise give it.]

Rule 1 – Application
a) These RULES shall APPLY TO ALL VESSELS UPON THE HIGH SEAS and in all waters connected therewith navigable by seagoing vessels.
b) Nothing in these rules shall interfere with the operation of special rules made by an appropriate authority for roadsteads, harbours, rivers, lakes or inland waterways connected with the high seas and navigable by seagoing vessels. Such special rules shall conform as closely as possible to these rules.

c) Nothing in these rules shall interfere with the operation of any special rules made by the government of any state with respect to additional station or signal lights or whistle signals for ships of war and vessels proceeding under convoy, or with respect to additional station or signal lights for fishing vessels engaged in fishing as a fleet.

d) Traffic separation schemes may be adopted by the Organisation for the purpose of these rules.

Rule 2 – Responsibility

a) Nothing in these rules shall exonerate any vessel or the owner, master or crew thereof, from the consequences of any neglect to comply with these rules or of the neglect of any precaution which may be required by the ordinary practice of seamen, or by the special circumstances of the case.

b) In construing and complying with these rules due regard shall be had to all dangers of navigation and collision and to any special circumstances, including the limitations of the vessels involved, which may make a departure from these rules necessary to avoid immediate danger. [In other words, pedantic adherence to the written rules is not enough, either at sea or in the courtroom.]

Rule 3 – General definitions

For the purpose of these rules, except where the context otherwise requires:

a) The word 'VESSEL' includes EVERY DESCRIPTION OF WATER CRAFT, including non-displacement craft and seaplanes, used or capable of being used as a means of transportation on water.

b) The term 'POWER-DRIVEN VESSEL' means any vessel PROPELLED BY MACHINERY.

c) The term 'SAILING VESSEL' means any vessel UNDER SAIL PROVIDED THAT PROPELLING MACHINERY, IF FITTED, IS NOT BEING USED.

d) The term 'VESSEL ENGAGED IN FISHING' means any vessel FISHING WITH NETS, LINES, TRAWLS OR OTHER FISHING APPARATUS WHICH RESTRICT MANOEUVRABILITY but does not include a vessel fishing with trolling lines or other fishing apparatus which do not restrict manoeuvrability.

f) The term 'VESSEL NOT UNDER COMMAND' means a vessel which through some exceptional circumstance is UNABLE TO MANOEUVRE AS REQUIRED BY THESE RULES and is therefore unable to keep out of the way of another vessel.

g) The term 'VESSEL RESTRICTED IN HER ABILITY TO MANOEUVRE' means a vessel which FROM THE NATURE OF HER WORK IS

Wake course or water track

RESTRICTED IN HER ABILITY TO MANOEUVRE AS REQUIRED by these rules and is therefore unable to keep out of the way of another vessel. The following vessels shall be regarded as vessels restricted in their ability to manoeuvre:

   (i) a vessel engaged in laying, servicing or picking up a navigation mark, submarine cable or pipeline

  (ii) a vessel engaged in dredging, surveying or underwater operations

 (iii) a vessel engaged in replenishment or transferring persons, provisions or cargo while under way

 (iv) a vessel engaged in the launching or recovery of aircraft

  (v) a vessel engaged in minesweeping operations

 (vi) a vessel engaged in a towing operation such as severely restricts the towing vessel and her tow in their ability to deviate from their course

h) The term 'VESSEL CONSTRAINED BY HER DRAUGHT' means a power-driven vessel which, because of her draught in relation to the available depth of water, is SEVERELY RESTRICTED IN HER ABILITY TO DEVIATE from the course she is following.

i) The term 'UNDER WAY' means that a vessel is NOT AT ANCHOR, OR MADE FAST TO THE SHORE, OR AGROUND.

k) Vessels shall be deemed to be in sight of one another only when one can be observed visually from the other.

l) The term 'RESTRICTED VISIBILITY' means any conditions in which VISIBILITY IS RESTRICTED BY FOG, MIST, FALLING SNOW, HEAVY RAINSTORMS, SANDSTORMS OR ANY OTHER SIMILAR CAUSES.

Part B – Steering and sailing rules

SECTION 1 – CONDUCT OF VESSELS IN ANY CONDITION OF VISIBILITY

[Some more definitions, a lot of good practical advice such as the need to make bold, visible changes of course when trying to avoid a collision, and the important **Rule 10** governing traffic separation schemes, without an understanding of which it would not be safe to navigate in the English Channel. The key message here is that a small sailing yacht must not 'impede the passage' of large commercial craft through such crowded waters. In some situations the law demands as much, and it always makes common sense.]

Rule 5 – Look-out

EVERY VESSEL shall AT ALL TIMES MAINTAIN A PROPER LOOK-OUT BY SIGHT AND HEARING as well as by all available means

● ● ●

appropriate in the prevailing circumstances and conditions SO AS TO MAKE A FULL APPRAISAL OF THE SITUATION AND THE RISK OF COLLISION.

Rule 6 – Safe speed

EVERY VESSEL shall at all times proceed at a SAFE SPEED so that she can take PROPER AND EFFECTIVE ACTION TO AVOID COLLISION and be STOPPED WITHIN A DISTANCE APPROPRIATE to the prevailing circumstances and conditions. In determining a safe speed the following factors shall be among those taken into account:

a) By all vessels:
  (i) the state of VISIBILITY
  (ii) the TRAFFIC DENSITY including concentrations of fishing vessels or any other vessels
  (iii) the MANOEUVRABILITY of the vessel with special reference to stopping distance and turning ability in the prevailing conditions
  (iv) at night the presence of BACKGROUND LIGHT such as from shore lights or from back scatter of her own lights
  (v) the STATE OF WIND, SEA AND CURRENT, and the proximity of navigational hazards
  (vi) the DRAUGHT in relation to the available depth of water

b) Additionally, by vessels with operational radar:
  (i) the characteristics, efficiency and limitations of the radar equipment
  (ii) any constraints imposed by the radar range scale in use
  (iii) the effect on radar detection of the sea state, weather and other sources of interference
  (iv) the possibility that small vessels, ice and other floating objects may not be detected by radar at an adequate range
  (v) the number, location and movement of vessels detected by radar
  (vi) the more exact assessment of the visibility that may be possible when radar is used to determine the range of vessels or other objects in the vicinity

Rule 7 – Risk of collision

a) Every vessel shall use all available means appropriate to the prevailing circumstances and conditions to determine if risk of collision exists. If there is any doubt such risk shall be deemed to exist.

b) Proper use shall be made of radar equipment if fitted and operational, including long-range scanning to obtain early warning of risk of collision and radar plotting or equivalent systematic observation of detected objects.

Sierra

c) Assumptions shall not be made on the basis of scanty information, especially scanty radar information.

d) In DETERMINING IF RISK OF COLLISION EXISTS the following considerations shall be among those taken into account:
  (i) such risk shall be deemed to exist IF THE COMPASS BEARING OF AN APPROACHING VESSEL DOES NOT APPRECIABLY CHANGE
  (ii) such risk may sometimes exist even when an appreciable bearing change is evident, particularly when approaching a very large vessel or a tow or when approaching a vessel at close range

Rule 8 – Action to avoid collision

a) Any ACTION TAKEN TO AVOID COLLISION shall, if the circumstances of the case admit, be POSITIVE, made IN AMPLE TIME and with due regard to the observance of good seamanship.

b) ANY ALTERATION OF COURSE AND/OR SPEED TO AVOID COLLISION shall, if the circumstances of the case permit, be LARGE ENOUGH TO BE READILY APPARENT TO ANOTHER VESSEL OBSERVING VISUALLY OR BY RADAR; a succession of small alterations of course and/or speed should be avoided.

Normally, to arrive at C a yachtsman would steer course AB to allow for the tide; the correct procedure, however, is to steer AC and, because of the tidal set, arrive at D.

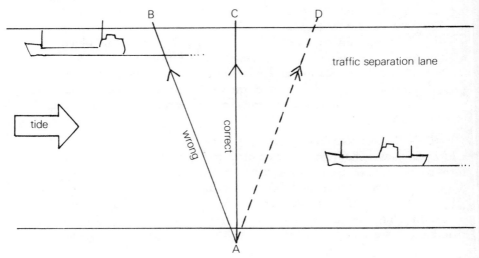

c) If there is sufficient sea room, alteration of course alone may be the most effective action to avoid a close-quarters situation provided that it is made in good time, is substantial and does not result in another close-quarters situation.

d) Action taken to avoid collision with another vessel shall be such as to result in passing at a safe distance. The effectiveness of the action shall be carefully checked until the other vessel is finally past and clear.

e) If necessary to avoid collision or allow more time to assess the situation, a vessel shall slacken her speed or take all way off by stopping or reversing her means of propulsion.

Rule 9 – Narrow channels
a) A VESSEL proceeding along the course of a narrow channel or fairway SHALL KEEP as near TO THE OUTER LIMIT OF THE CHANNEL OR FAIRWAY WHICH LIES ON HER STARBOARD SIDE as is safe and practicable.

b) *A vessel of less than 20 metres in length or a SAILING VESSEL SHALL NOT IMPEDE THE PASSAGE OF A VESSEL WHICH CAN SAFELY NAVIGATE ONLY WITHIN A NARROW CHANNEL OR FAIRWAY.*

c) A VESSEL ENGAGED IN FISHING SHALL NOT IMPEDE THE PASSAGE OF ANY OTHER VESSEL navigating within a narrow channel or fairway.

d) A VESSEL SHALL NOT CROSS A NARROW CHANNEL OR FAIR-WAY IF SUCH CROSSING IMPEDES the passage of a vessel which can safely navigate only within such channel or fairway. The latter vessel may use the sound signal prescribed in **Rule 34d** [five short and rapid blasts] if in doubt as to the intention of the crossing vessel.

e) (i) In a narrow channel or fairway when overtaking can take place only if the vessel to be overtaken takes action to permit safe passing, the VESSEL INTENDING TO OVERTAKE shall indicate her intention by sounding the appropriate signal prescribed in **Rule 34c (i)** [TWO LONG AND ONE SHORT BLAST IF OVERTAKING TO STAR-BOARD; TWO LONG AND TWO SHORT TO PORT]. The VESSEL TO BE OVERTAKEN shall, IF IN AGREEMENT, sound the appropriate signal prescribed in **Rule 34c (ii)** [A SERIES OF BLASTS – LONG, SHORT, LONG AND SHORT] and take steps to permit safe passing. IF IN DOUBT she may sound the signals prescribed in **Rule 34d** [FIVE SHORT AND RAPID BLASTS]

(ii) This rule does not relieve the overtaking vessel of her obligation under **Rule 13** [to keep clear of the vessel being overtaken]

Quebec

f) A VESSEL NEARING A BEND or an area of a narrow channel or fairway where other vessels may be obscured by an intervening obstruction shall navigate with particular alertness and caution and shall sound the appropriate signal prescribed in **Rule 34e** [ONE LONG BLAST].

g) ANY VESSEL shall, if the circumstances of the case admit, AVOID ANCHORING in a narrow channel.

Rule 10 – Traffic separation schemes

a) This rule applies to traffic separation schemes adopted by the Organisation.

b) A VESSEL USING A TRAFFIC SEPARATION SCHEME shall:
  - (i) PROCEED in the appropriate traffic lane IN THE GENERAL DIRECTION OF TRAFFIC FLOW for that lane
  - (ii) so far as practicable KEEP CLEAR OF A TRAFFIC SEPARATION LANE or separation zone
  - (iii) NORMALLY JOIN OR LEAVE a traffic lane AT THE TERMINATION of the lane, but WHEN JOINING OR LEAVING FROM THE SIDE shall do so AT AS SMALL AN ANGLE TO THE GENERAL DIRECTION OF TRAFFIC FLOW AS PRACTICABLE

c) A VESSEL shall so far as practicable avoid crossing traffic lanes, but if obliged to do so shall CROSS AS NEARLY AS PRACTICABLE AT RIGHT ANGLES TO THE GENERAL DIRECTION OF THE TRAFFIC FLOW.

[A slow moving yacht being set sideways by a strong tidal stream while crossing a separation scheme should if possible steer a course at right angles to the traffic flow so as to reach the far side as quickly as possible, not head uptide so as to make good a right-angled course. Coastguards who may be watching the yacht's progress by radar will, or at least should, make allowance for the tidal effect. The phrase 'as nearly as practicable' in this rule also covers a sailing yacht's inability to sail directly into the wind.]

d) INSHORE TRAFFIC ZONES shall NOT NORMALLY BE USED BY THROUGH TRAFFIC which can safely use the appropriate traffic lane within the adjacent traffic separation scheme.

e) A VESSEL, OTHER THAN A CROSSING VESSEL, SHALL NOT NORMALLY ENTER a separation zone or cross a separation line EXCEPT:
  - (i) in cases of EMERGENCY to avoid immediate danger
  - (ii) to engage in FISHING within a separation zone

f) A VESSEL navigating in areas NEAR THE TERMINATION of traffic separation schemes shall do so with PARTICULAR CAUTION.

g) A VESSEL shall so far as practicable AVOID ANCHORING in a traffic separation scheme or in areas near its terminations.

h) A VESSEL NOT USING a traffic separation scheme shall AVOID IT by as wide a margin as is practicable.

i) A VESSEL ENGAGED IN FISHING SHALL NOT IMPEDE the passage of any vessel following a traffic lane.

j) A vessel of less than 20 metres in length or a SAILING VESSEL SHALL NOT IMPEDE THE SAFE PASSAGE OF A POWER-DRIVEN VESSEL following a traffic lane.

SECTION II – CONDUCT OF VESSELS IN SIGHT OF ONE ANOTHER

Rule 12 – Sailing vessels

a) When TWO SAILING VESSELS ARE APPROACHING ONE ANOTHER, so as to involve the risk of collision, one of them shall keep out of the way of the other as follows:

    (i) when each has the WIND ON A DIFFERENT SIDE, the vessel which has the wind on the PORT SIDE SHALL KEEP OUT OF THE WAY of the other

    (ii) when both have the WIND ON THE SAME SIDE, the vessel which is to WINDWARD SHALL KEEP OUT OF THE WAY of the vessel which is to leeward

    (iii) if a vessel with the wind on the port side sees a vessel to windward and CANNOT DETERMINE WITH CERTAINTY whether the other vessel has the wind on the port or the starboard side, she shall KEEP OUT OF THE WAY of the other

b) For the purposes of this rule the WINDWARD SIDE shall be deemed to be the SIDE OPPOSITE TO THAT ON WHICH THE MAINSAIL IS CARRIED or, in the case of a square-rigged vessel, the side opposite to that on which the largest fore-and-aft sail is carried.

Rule 13 – Overtaking

a) Notwithstanding anything contained in the rules of this section ANY VESSEL OVERTAKING any other shall KEEP OUT OF THE WAY of the vessel being overtaken.

b) A VESSEL shall be deemed to be OVERTAKING WHEN COMING UP WITH ANOTHER VESSEL FROM A DIRECTION MORE THAN 22.5° ABAFT HER BEAM, that is, in such a position with reference to the vessel she is overtaking that AT NIGHT SHE WOULD BE ABLE TO SEE ONLY THE STERNLIGHT of that vessel but neither of her sidelights.

Number one

c) When a vessel is in doubt as to whether she is overtaking another, she shall assume that this is the case and act accordingly. [Note the principle, also applied in **Rule 12a (iii)**, and in **Rule 14c** below, that if in doubt you keep clear.]

d) Any subsequent alteration of the bearing between the two vessels shall not make the overtaking vessel a crossing vessel within the meaning of these rules or relieve her of the duty of keeping clear of the overtaken vessel until she is finally past and clear. [The disastrous collision off the Isle of Wight in 1970, between the Liberian tankers *Pacific Glory* and *Allegro*, involved the potential conflict – referred to here – between the overtaking rule and the crossing situation covered by **Rule 15** below.]

Rule 14 – Head-on situation

a) When TWO POWER-DRIVEN VESSELS ARE MEETING ON RECIPROCAL OR NEARLY RECIPROCAL COURSES so as to involve risk of collision EACH SHALL ALTER HER COURSE TO STARBOARD so that each shall pass on the port side of the other.

b) Such a situation shall be deemed to exist when a vessel sees the other ahead or nearly ahead and by night she can see the masthead lights of the other in a line or nearly in a line and/or both sidelights, and by day she observes the corresponding aspect of the other vessel.

c) When a vessel is in any doubt as to whether such a situation exists she shall assume that it does and act accordingly. [Generations of seamen have learnt this rule by memorizing Thomas Gray's verses:

> When you see three lights ahead,
> Starboard wheel and show your Red.
> Green to Green or Red to Red,
> Perfect safety, go ahead.]

Rule 15 – Crossing situation

When TWO POWER-DRIVEN VESSELS ARE CROSSING so as to involve risk of collision, the VESSEL WHICH HAS THE OTHER ON HER OWN STARBOARD SIDE SHALL KEEP OUT OF THE WAY and shall, if the circumstances of the case admit, avoid crossing ahead of the other vessel. [The Thomas Gray version goes like this:

> If to your starboard Red appear,
> It is your duty to keep clear,
> To act as judgment says is proper,
> To port, or starboard, back or stop her.
> But when upon your port is seen

A steamer's starboard light of Green,
There's not so much for you to do;
The green light must keep clear of you.]

Rule 16 – Action by give-way vessel
EVERY VESSEL WHICH IS DIRECTED TO KEEP OUT OF THE WAY of another vessel shall, so far as possible, take EARLY AND SUBSTANTIAL ACTION to keep well clear.

Rule 17 – Action by stand-on vessel
a) (i) Where one of two vessels is to keep out of the way THE OTHER SHALL KEEP HER COURSE AND SPEED
   (ii) The LATTER MAY HOWEVER TAKE ACTION TO AVOID COLLISION BY HER MANOEUVRE ALONE as soon as it becomes apparent to her that the vessel required to keep out of the way is NOT TAKING APPROPRIATE ACTION IN COMPLIANCE WITH THESE RULES
b) When, from any cause, the VESSEL REQUIRED TO KEEP HER COURSE AND SPEED finds herself SO CLOSE THAT COLLISION CANNOT BE AVOIDED BY THE ACTION OF THE GIVE-WAY VESSEL ALONE, she shall take SUCH ACTION AS WILL BEST AID TO AVOID COLLISION. [The careful wording of this rule, though perhaps confusing, is vital in some collision situations between large vessels. Small yachts should try to apply the more basic rules of self preservation.]
c) A POWER-DRIVEN VESSEL WHICH TAKES ACTION IN A CROSSING SITUATION in accordance with sub-paragraph a(ii) of this rule to avoid collision with another power-driven vessel shall, if the circumstances of the case permit, NOT ALTER COURSE TO PORT FOR A VESSEL ON HER OWN PORT SIDE.
d) This rule does not relieve the give-way vessel of her obligation to keep out of the way.

Rule 18 – Responsibilities between vessels
[The following maritime 'pecking order' is obvious examination material and worth learning as such. Remember that an auxiliary sailing yacht is a 'power-driven vessel' as defined by **Rule 3** when her engine is being used.]
Except where **Rules 9, 10** and **13** otherwise require
a) A POWER-DRIVEN VESSEL UNDER WAY shall keep out of the way of:
   (i) A VESSEL NOT UNDER COMMAND

V Qk Fl or Qk Fl

(ii) A VESSEL RESTRICTED IN HER ABILITY TO MANOEUVRE
(iii) A VESSEL ENGAGED IN FISHING
(iv) A SAILING VESSEL

b) A SAILING VESSEL UNDER WAY shall keep out of the way of:
(i) A VESSEL NOT UNDER COMMAND
(ii) A VESSEL RESTRICTED IN HER ABILITY TO MANOEUVRE
(iii) A VESSEL ENGAGED IN FISHING

c) A VESSEL ENGAGED IN FISHING WHEN UNDER WAY shall, so far as possible, keep out of the way of:
(i) A VESSEL NOT UNDER COMMAND
(ii) A VESSEL RESTRICTED IN HER ABILITY TO MANOEUVRE

d) (i) ANY VESSEL OTHER THAN A VESSEL NOT UNDER COMMAND OR A VESSEL RESTRICTED IN HER ABILITY TO MANOEUVRE shall, if the circumstances of the case admit, avoid impeding the safe passage of a VESSEL CONSTRAINED BY HER DRAUGHT, exhibiting the signals in **Rule 28** [three all-round red lights in a vertical line, or a cylinder]
(ii) A vessel constrained by her draught shall navigate with particular caution having full regard to her special condition

e) A seaplane on the water shall, in general, keep well clear of all vessels and avoid impeding their navigation.

SECTION III – CONDUCT OF VESSELS IN RESTRICTED VISIBILITY
[A section of the rules not always obeyed in practice and one under which the relatively privileged legal position still enjoyed by small sailing craft is more than usually artificial.]

a) This rule applies to vessels not in sight of one another when navigating in or near an area of restricted visibility.

b) EVERY VESSEL shall proceed AT A SAFE SPEED ADAPTED TO THE PREVAILING CIRCUMSTANCES and conditions of restricted visibility. A power-driven vessel shall have her engines ready for immediate manoeuvre.

d) A vessel which detects by radar alone the presence of another vessel shall determine if a close-quarters situation is developing and/or risk of collision exists. If so, she shall take avoiding action in ample time, provided that when such action consists of an alteration of course, so far as possible the following shall be avoided:
(i) an alteration of course to port for a vessel forward of the beam, other than for a vessel being overtaken
(ii) an alteration of course towards a vessel abeam or abaft the beam

e) Except where it has been determined that a risk of collision does not exist, EVERY VESSEL WHICH HEARS APPARENTLY FORWARD OF HER BEAM THE FOG SIGNAL OF ANOTHER VESSEL, or which cannot avoid a close-quarters situation with another vessel forward of her beam, shall REDUCE HER SPEED TO THE MINIMUM AT WHICH SHE CAN BE KEPT ON HER COURSE. She shall IF NECESSARY TAKE ALL HER WAY OFF and in any event navigate with extreme caution until danger of collision is over.

Part C – Lights and shapes
[Laid out merely as a mass of overlapping regulations, the IMCO rules on lights and shapes can look dreadfully confusing. But by a process of logical grouping and elimination, which we have tried to apply in the illustrations, they can be made manageable. After all, every one of them, from the multi-coloured array that makes a dredger look like a floating Christmas tree to the solitary white light displayed by a small sailing boat, has been devised to convey information and prevent collisions.

Of the five colours, two can quickly be disposed of because they so rarely occur. The blue is only shown when towing a Dracone. A steady yellow light is confined to tugs, to be shown above their normal white sternlight to avoid confusion with the tow's sternlight. A hovercraft uses a flashing yellow light, dashing along like a seagoing police car, and a vessel fishing with a purse seine net may show a pair of alternately flashing yellow lights if she is hampered by her gear. Apart from these few cases we are dealing with combinations of red, green and white. And the first distinction to make here is between directional lights that are meant to convey a perspective of movement through the darkness, and all-round lights which generally tell you what sort of vessel you can see – whether she is moving or not – and the situation she is in.

A ship's basic navigation lights, for example, consist of red and green lights showing respectively to port and starboard, and a pair of forward facing white masthead lights (or perhaps only one if the vessel is less than 50 metres long) with the rear one set higher than the other so you can tell instantly which way she is heading. On the other hand the additional green and white lights shown by a fishing trawler – whether she is under way or not – are visible all round. So are the white and red lights carried by a pilot cutter (same colours as the pilot flag H), or the two reds shown by a vessel not under command. The colour red, you will notice, is generally associated with situations of difficulty or danger – vessels aground, manoeuvring with difficulty, constrained by their draught and so on.

Whisky

Another principle running through the IMCO system is that you add lights as the vessel, or combination of vessels, gets larger. A small tug on her own may show just the single white masthead light for instance. If she is more than 50 metres long she must carry a second, similar, light aft. When towing, the forward light is doubled up, and if the length of the tow exceeds 200 metres she adds a third. Seen from ahead, therefore, she will by now present a vertical line of four white masthead lights, plus the red and green sidelights to port and starboard.]

Rule 20 – Application
b) The rules concerning lights shall be complied with from sunset to sunrise, and during such times no other lights shall be exhibited, except such lights as cannot be mistaken for the lights specified in these rules or do not impair their visibility or distinctive character, or interfere with the keeping of a proper look-out.

Rule 21 – Definitions
a) 'MASTHEAD LIGHT' means a white light placed over the fore and aft centreline of the vessel showing an unbroken light OVER AN ARC OF THE HORIZON of 225° and so fixed as to show the light from right ahead to 22.5° abaft the beam on either side of the vessel (see plate 3).
b) 'SIDELIGHTS' means a green light on the starboard side and a red light on the port side each showing an unbroken light OVER AN ARC OF THE HORIZON OF 112.5° and so fixed as to show the light from right ahead to 22.5° abaft the beam on its respective side. In a vessel of less than 20 metres in length the sidelights may be combined in one lantern carried on the fore and aft centreline of the vessel.
c) 'STERNLIGHT' means a white light placed as nearly as practicable at the stern showing an unbroken light OVER AN ARC OF THE HORIZON OF 135° and so fixed as to show the light 67.5° from right aft on each side of the vessel.
d) 'Towing light' means a yellow light having the same characteristics as the sternlight.
e) 'All-round light' means a light showing an unbroken light over an arc of the horizon of 360°.
f) 'Flashing light' means a light flashing at regular intervals at a frequency of 120 flashes or more per minute.

Rule 22 – Visibility of lights
a) In vessels of 50 metres or more in length:

masthead light – 6 miles
sidelight – 3 miles
sternlight – 3 miles
towing light – 3 miles
all-round light of any colour – 3 miles
b) In vessels 12 to 50 metres long:
masthead light – 5 miles [but only 3 miles if the vessel is less than 20 metres long)
sidelight – 2 miles
sternlight – 2 miles
towing lights – 2 miles
all-round light of any colour – 2 miles
c) In vessels less than 12 metres long:
masthead light – 2 miles
sidelight – 1 mile
sternlight – 2 miles
towing light – 2 miles
all-round light of any colour – 2 miles

Rule 23 – Power-driven vessels under way
a) A POWER-DRIVEN VESSEL UNDER WAY shall exhibit:
  (i) a MASTHEAD LIGHT forward
  (ii) a SECOND MASTHEAD LIGHT abaft of and higher than the forward one, EXCEPT THAT A VESSEL OF LESS THAN 50 METRES IN LENGTH SHALL NOT BE OBLIGED TO EXHIBIT SUCH LIGHT, BUT MAY DO SO
  (iii) SIDELIGHTS
  (iv) a STERNLIGHT (see plate 4)
b) An AIR-CUSHION VESSEL when operating in the non-displacement mode shall, in addition to the lights prescribed in paragraph a of this rule, exhibit an ALL-ROUND FLASHING YELLOW LIGHT.
c) A POWER-DRIVEN VESSEL OF LESS THAN 7 METRES IN LENGTH and whose maximum speed does not exceed 7 knots may, in lieu of the lights prescribed in paragraph a of this rule, exhibit an ALL-ROUND WHITE LIGHT. Such vessels shall, if practicable, also exhibit sidelights.

Rule 24 – Towing and pushing
a) A POWER-DRIVEN VESSEL WHEN TOWING shall exhibit:
  (i) instead of the light prescribed in **Rule 23a(i)** [that is, the forward masthead light], TWO MASTHEAD LIGHTS FORWARD in a

Delta

vertical line; WHEN THE LENGTH OF THE TOW, measuring from the stern of the towing vessel to the after end of the tow, EXCEEDS 200 METRES, THREE SUCH LIGHTS in a vertical line
- (ii) SIDELIGHTS
- (iii) a STERNLIGHT
- (iv) a TOWING LIGHT in a vertical line ABOVE THE STERNLIGHT
- (v) WHEN THE LENGTH OF THE TOW EXCEEDS 200 METRES, A DIAMOND SHAPE (by day) where it can best be seen

[In other words, the characteristics of a tug at night are the extra masthead light or lights when seen from ahead and, usually, the yellow towing light seen from astern.]

b) When a pushing vessel and a vessel being pushed ahead are rigidly connected in a composite unit they shall be regarded as a power-driven vessel and exhibit the lights prescribed in **Rule 23**.

c) A POWER-DRIVEN VESSEL WHEN PUSHING AHEAD OR TOWING ALONGSIDE, except in the case of a composite unit, shall exhibit:
- (i) instead of the light prescribed in **Rule 23a(i)** [that is, the forward masthead light], TWO MASTHEAD LIGHTS FORWARD in a vertical line
- (ii) SIDELIGHTS
- (iii) a STERNLIGHT

[Note the absence of the yellow towing light in this case.]

d) A power-driven vessel to which paragraphs a and c of this rule apply shall also comply with **Rule 23a(ii)** [covering the second masthead light aft].

e) A VESSEL BEING TOWED shall exhibit:
- (i) SIDELIGHTS
- (ii) a STERNLIGHT
- (iii) when the length of the tow exceeds 200 metres, a diamond shape where it can best be seen

f) Provided that any number of vessels being towed alongside or pushed in a group shall be lighted as one vessel:
- (i) a vessel being pushed ahead, not being part of a composite unit, shall exhibit at the forward end, sidelights
- (ii) a vessel being towed alongside shall exhibit a sternlight and at the forward end, sidelights

g) Where from any sufficient cause it is impracticable for a vessel or object being towed to exhibit the lights prescribed in paragraph e of this rule, all possible measures shall be taken to light the vessel or object towed or at least to indicate the presence of the unlighted vessel or object.

Rule 25 – Sailing vessels under way and vessels under oars
a) A SAILING VESSEL UNDER WAY shall exhibit:
  (i) SIDELIGHTS
  (ii) a STERNLIGHT
b) In a SAILING VESSEL OF LESS THAN 12 METRES in length the LIGHTS prescribed in paragraph a of this rule MAY BE COMBINED IN ONE LANTERN carried at or near the top of the mast where it can best be seen.
c) A SAILING VESSEL UNDER WAY may, in addition to the lights prescribed in paragraph a of this rule, exhibit at or near the top of the mast, where they can best be seen, TWO ALL-ROUND LIGHTS IN A VERTICAL LINE, THE UPPER BEING RED AND THE LOWER GREEN, but these lights shall not be exhibited in conjunction with the combined lantern permitted by paragraph b of this rule.
d) (i) A SAILING VESSEL OF LESS THAN 7 METRES in length shall, if practicable, exhibit the lights prescribed in paragraph a or b of this rule, but if she does not, she shall have ready AN ELECTRIC TORCH OR LIGHTED LANTERN SHOWING A WHITE LIGHT which shall be exhibited in sufficient time to prevent collision.
  (ii) A VESSEL UNDER OARS may exhibit the lights prescribed in this rule for sailing vessels, but if she does not, she shall have ready at hand AN ELECTRIC TORCH OR LIGHTED LANTERN SHOWING A WHITE LIGHT which shall be exhibited in sufficient time to prevent collision.
e) A VESSEL PROCEEDING UNDER SAIL (in daylight) WHEN ALSO BEING PROPELLED BY MACHINERY shall exhibit forward where it can best be seen A CONICAL SHAPE APEX DOWNWARDS.

Rule 26 – Fishing vessels
b) A VESSEL WHEN ENGAGED IN TRAWLING (see plate 5), by which is meant the dragging through the water of a dredge net or other apparatus used as a fishing appliance, shall exhibit:
  (i) TWO ALL-ROUND LIGHTS IN A VERTICAL LINE, THE UPPER BEING GREEN AND THE LOWER WHITE, or a shape (by day) consisting of TWO CONES WITH THEIR APEXES TOGETHER in a vertical line one above the other; A VESSEL OF LESS THAN 20 METRES in length may instead of this shape exhibit a BASKET
  (ii) a MASTHEAD LIGHT ABAFT OF AND HIGHER THAN THE ALL-ROUND GREEN LIGHT; a vessel of less than 50 metres in length shall not be obliged to exhibit such a light but may do so

Zulu

(iii) WHEN MAKING WAY THROUGH THE WATER, in addition to the lights prescribed in this paragraph, SIDELIGHTS AND A STERNLIGHT

[Note that the single green all-round light is characteristic of the trawler, although a dredger and a minesweeper may show two or three green lights respectively.]

c) A VESSEL ENGAGED IN FISHING OTHER THAN TRAWLING shall exhibit:

(i) TWO ALL-ROUND LIGHTS IN A VERTICAL LINE, THE UPPER BEING RED AND THE LOWER WHITE, or a shape (by day) consisting of TWO CONES WITH APEXES TOGETHER in a vertical line one above the other; A VESSEL OF LESS THAN 20 METRES may instead of this shape exhibit a BASKET

(ii) when there is OUTLYING GEAR extending more than 150 metres horizontally from the vessel, an ALL-ROUND WHITE LIGHT OR CONE APEX UPWARDS (by day) IN THE DIRECTION OF THE GEAR

(iii) WHEN MAKING WAY THROUGH THE WATER, in addition to the lights prescribed in this paragraph, SIDELIGHTS AND A STERNLIGHT

d) A VESSEL ENGAGED IN FISHING IN CLOSE PROXIMITY TO OTHER VESSELS engaged in fishing may exhibit the ADDITIONAL SIGNALS described in Annex II to these regulations (see page 81).

e) A VESSEL WHEN NOT ENGAGED IN FISHING SHALL NOT EXHIBIT THE LIGHTS or shapes prescribed in this rule, but only those prescribed for a vessel of her length.

Rule 27 – Vessels not under command or restricted in their ability to manoeuvre

a) A VESSEL NOT UNDER COMMAND (see plate 6) shall exhibit:

(i) TWO ALL-ROUND RED LIGHTS in a vertical line where they can best be seen

(ii) TWO BALLS (by day) or similar shapes in a vertical line where they can best be seen

(iii) WHEN MAKING WAY THROUGH THE WATER, in addition to the lights prescribed in this paragraph, SIDELIGHTS AND A STERNLIGHT

b) A VESSEL RESTRICTED IN HER ABILITY TO MANOEUVRE, except a vessel engaged in minesweeping operations, shall exhibit:

(i) THREE ALL-ROUND LIGHTS in a vertical line where they can best be seen. The HIGHEST AND LOWEST of these lights shall be RED and the MIDDLE light shall be WHITE

(ii) THREE SHAPES (by day) in a vertical line where they can best be seen. The HIGHEST AND LOWEST of these shapes shall be BALLS and the MIDDLE one a diamond

(iii) WHEN MAKING WAY THROUGH THE WATER, MASTHEAD LIGHTS, SIDELIGHTS AND A STERNLIGHT, in addition to the lights prescribed in sub-paragraph (i)

(iv) when AT ANCHOR, in addition to the lights or shapes prescribed in sub-paragraphs (i) and (ii), the lights or shape prescribed in **Rule 30** [AT LEAST ONE ALL-ROUND WHITE LIGHT FORWARD OR A SINGLE BALL]

c) A vessel engaged in a towing operation such as renders her unable to deviate from her course shall, in addition to the lights or shapes prescribed in sub-paragraphs b(i) and (ii) of this rule, exhibit the lights or shape prescribed in **Rule 24a** [extra masthead light or lights forward, and towing light aft, or diamond shape].

d) A VESSEL ENGAGED IN DREDGING OR UNDERWATER OPERA-TIONS, when restricted in her ability to manoeuvre, shall exhibit the lights and shapes prescribed in paragraphs b of this rule and shall in addition, when an obstruction exists, exhibit:

(i) TWO ALL-ROUND RED LIGHTS OR TWO BALLS in a vertical line to indicate the SIDE ON WHICH THE OBSTRUCTION EXISTS

(ii) TWO ALL-ROUND GREEN LIGHTS OR TWO DIAMONDS in a vertical line to indicate the SIDE ON WHICH ANOTHER VESSEL MAY PASS

(iii) WHEN MAKING WAY THROUGH THE WATER, in addition to the lights prescribed in this paragraph, MASTHEAD LIGHTS, SIDELIGHTS AND A STERNLIGHT

(iv) a vessel to which this paragraph applies when at anchor shall exhibit the lights or shapes prescribed in paragraphs (i) and (ii) instead of the lights or shape prescribed in **Rule 30**

e) Whenever the size of a vessel engaged in diving operations makes it impracticable to exhibit the shapes prescribed in paragraph d of this rule, a rigid replica of the International Code flag A not less than 1 metre in height shall be exhibited. Measures shall be taken to ensure all-round visibility.

f) A VESSEL ENGAGED IN MINESWEEPING OPERATIONS shall, in

addition to the lights prescribed for a power-driven vessel in **Rule 23** [masthead lights, sidelights and sternlight], exhibit THREE ALL-ROUND GREEN LIGHTS OR THREE BALLS. One of these lights or shapes shall be exhibited at or near the foremast head and one at each end of the fore yard. These lights or shapes indicate that it is dangerous for another vessel to approach closer than 1000 metres astern or 500 metres on either side of the minesweeper.

g) Vessels of less than 7 metres in length shall not be required to exhibit the lights prescribed in this rule.

Rule 28 – Vessels constrained by their draught

A VESSEL CONSTRAINED BY HER DRAUGHT (see plate 7) may, in addition to the lights prescribed for power-driven vessels in **Rule 23** [masthead lights, sidelights and sternlight], exhibit where they can best be seen THREE ALL-ROUND RED LIGHTS in a vertical line, or (by day) a CYLINDER.

Rule 29 – Pilot vessels

a) A VESSEL ENGAGED ON PILOTAGE DUTY shall exhibit:
  - (i) at or near the masthead, TWO ALL-ROUND LIGHTS in a vertical line, the UPPER BEING WHITE AND THE LOWER RED [compare the white and red pilot flag]
  - (ii) WHEN UNDER WAY, in addition, SIDELIGHTS AND A STERN-LIGHT
  - (iii) when AT ANCHOR, in addition to the lights prescribed in sub-paragraph (i), the ANCHOR LIGHT, LIGHTS OR SHAPE

b) A pilot vessel when not engaged on pilotage duty shall exhibit the lights or shapes prescribed for a similar vessel of her length.

Rule 30 – Anchored vessels and vessels aground

a) A VESSEL AT ANCHOR shall exhibit where it can best be seen:
  - (i) IN THE FORE PART, AN ALL-ROUND WHITE LIGHT OR ONE BALL
  - (ii) AT OR NEAR THE STERN AND AT A LOWER LEVEL than the light prescribed in sub-paragraph (i), AN ALL-ROUND WHITE LIGHT

b) A VESSEL OF LESS THAN 50 METRES in length may exhibit AN ALL-ROUND WHITE LIGHT where it can best be seen instead of the lights prescribed in paragraph a of this rule.

c) A vessel at anchor may, and A VESSEL OF 100 METRES AND MORE in length shall, ALSO USE THE AVAILABLE WORKING OR EQUIVA-LENT LIGHTS to illuminate her decks.

d) A VESSEL AGROUND shall exhibit the lights prescribed in paragraph a or b of this rule and IN ADDITION, where they can best be seen:

(i) TWO ALL-ROUND RED LIGHTS in a vertical line

(ii) THREE BALLS in a vertical line

e) A VESSEL OF LESS THAN 7 METRES in length, when at anchor or aground, NOT IN OR NEAR A NARROW CHANNEL, FAIRWAY OR ANCHORAGE, OR WHERE OTHER VESSELS NORMALLY NAVI-GATE, SHALL NOT BE REQUIRED TO EXHIBIT THE LIGHTS OR SHAPES prescribed in paragraphs a, b or d of this rule.

Part D – Sound and light signals

Rule 32 – Definitions

a) The word 'whistle' means any sound signalling appliance capable of producing the prescribed blasts and which complies with the specifications of Annex III.

b) The term 'SHORT BLAST' means a blast of ABOUT ONE SECOND'S DURATION.

c) The term 'PROLONGED BLAST' means a blast of FROM FOUR TO SIX SECONDS' DURATION.

Rule 33 – Equipment for sound signals

a) A VESSEL OF 12 METRES OR MORE in length shall be provided with a WHISTLE AND A BELL and a VESSEL OF 100 METRES OR MORE in length shall, IN ADDITION, be provided with a GONG, the tone and sound of which cannot be confused with that of the bell.

b) A VESSEL OF LESS THAN 12 METRES in length SHALL NOT BE OBLIGED TO CARRY THE SOUND SIGNALLING APPLIANCES prescribed in paragraph a of this rule, but IF SHE DOES NOT, she shall be provided with SOME OTHER MEANS OF MAKING AN EFFICIENT SOUND SIGNAL.

Rule 34 – Manoeuvring and warning signals

a) When vessels are in sight of one another, a POWER-DRIVEN VESSEL UNDER WAY, when manoeuvring as authorized or required by these rules, shall indicate that manoeuvre by the following signals on her whistle:

ONE SHORT BLAST – 'I AM ALTERING MY COURSE TO STAR-BOARD'

TWO SHORT BLASTS – 'I AM ALTERING MY COURSE TO PORT'

November

THREE SHORT BLASTS – 'I AM OPERATING ASTERN PRO-PULSION'

b) Any vessel may supplement the whistle signals prescribed in paragraph a of this rule by light signals, repeated as appropriate, whilst the manoeuvre is being carried out:

(i) ONE FLASH (Morse letter E) – 'I AM ALTERING MY COURSE TO STARBOARD'
TWO FLASHES (Morse letter I) – 'I AM ALTERING MY COURSE TO PORT'
THREE FLASHES (Morse letter S) – 'I AM OPERATING ASTERN PROPULSION'

(ii) the duration of each flash shall be about one second, the interval between flashes shall be about one second, and the interval between successive signals shall be not less than ten seconds

c) When in sight of one another in a narrow channel or fairway:

(i) A VESSEL INTENDING TO OVERTAKE another shall in compliance with **Rule 13** indicate her intention by the following signals on her whistle:
TWO PROLONGED BLASTS FOLLOWED BY ONE SHORT BLAST – 'I INTEND TO OVERTAKE YOU ON YOUR STARBOARD SIDE'
TWO PROLONGED BLASTS FOLLOWED BY TWO SHORT BLASTS – 'I INTEND TO OVERTAKE YOU ON YOUR PORT SIDE'

(ii) the VESSEL ABOUT TO BE OVERTAKEN when acting in accordance with **Rule 9e(i)** shall INDICATE AGREEMENT BY the following signal on her whistle:
ONE PROLONGED, ONE SHORT, ONE PROLONGED AND ONE SHORT BLAST, in that order

d) When vessels in sight of one another are approaching each other and from any cause EITHER VESSEL FAILS TO UNDERSTAND THE INTENTIONS OR ACTIONS OF THE OTHER, OR IS IN DOUBT WHETHER SUFFICIENT ACTION IS BEING TAKEN TO AVOID COLLISION, the vessel in doubt shall immediately indicate such doubt by giving AT LEAST FIVE SHORT AND RAPID BLASTS on the whistle. Such signal may be supplemented by a LIGHT SIGNAL OF AT LEAST FIVE SHORT AND RAPID FLASHES.

e) A VESSEL NEARING A BEND or an area of a channel or fairway WHERE OTHER VESSELS MAY BE OBSCURED by an intervening obstruction shall sound ONE PROLONGED BLAST. Such signal shall be ANSWERED WITH A PROLONGED BLAST by any approaching vessel that may be within hearing around the bend or behind the intervening obstruction.

Rule 35 – Sound signals in restricted visibility
In or near an area of restricted visibility, whether by day or night, the signals prescribed by this rule shall be used as follows:
a) A POWER-DRIVEN VESSEL MAKING WAY THROUGH THE WATER shall sound at INTERVALS OF NOT MORE THAN 2 MINUTES ONE PROLONGED BLAST.
b) A POWER-DRIVEN VESSEL UNDER WAY BUT STOPPED and making no way through the water shall sound at intervals of not more than 2 minutes TWO PROLONGED BLASTS in succession with an interval of about 2 seconds between them.
c) A VESSEL NOT UNDER COMMAND, A VESSEL RESTRICTED IN HER ABILITY TO MANOEUVRE, A VESSEL CONSTRAINED BY HER DRAUGHT, A SAILING VESSEL, A VESSEL ENGAGED IN FISHING AND A VESSEL ENGAGED IN TOWING OR PUSHING another vessel shall, instead of the signals prescribed in paragraphs a or b of this rule, sound at intervals of not more than 2 minutes three blasts in succession, namely ONE PROLONGED FOLLOWED BY TWO SHORT BLASTS.
d) A VESSEL TOWED, or if more than one vessel is towed the last vessel of the tow, if manned, shall at intervals of not more than 2 minutes sound four blasts in succession, namely ONE PROLONGED FOLLOWED BY THREE SHORT BLASTS. When practicable, this signal shall be made immediately after the signal made by the towing vessel.
e) When a pushing vessel and a vessel being pushed ahead are rigidly connected in a composite unit they shall be regarded as a power-driven vessel and shall give the signals prescribed in paragraphs a or b of this rule.
f) A VESSEL AT ANCHOR shall AT INTERVALS OF NOT MORE THAN ONE MINUTE RING THE BELL RAPIDLY FOR ABOUT 5 SECONDS. In a VESSEL OF 100 METRES OR MORE in length the bell shall be sounded in the fore part of the vessel and IMMEDIATELY AFTER THE RINGING OF THE BELL THE GONG SHALL BE SOUNDED RAPIDLY FOR ABOUT 5 SECONDS IN THE AFTER PART OF THE VESSEL. A vessel at anchor may in addition sound three blasts in succession, namely one short, one prolonged and one short blast, to give warning of her position and the possibility of collision to an approaching vessel.

Charlie

g) A VESSEL AGROUND shall give the bell signal and if required the gong signal prescribed in paragraph f of this rule and shall, IN ADDITION, give THREE SEPARATE AND DISTINCT STROKES ON THE BELL IMMEDIATELY BEFORE AND AFTER THE RAPID RINGING OF THE BELL. A vessel aground may in addition sound an appropriate whistle signal.

h) A VESSEL OF LESS THAN 12 METRES in length shall not be obliged to give the above-mentioned signals but, if she does not, shall make SOME OTHER EFFICIENT SOUND SIGNAL at intervals of not more than 2 minutes.

i) A PILOT VESSEL when engaged on pilotage duty may in addition to the signals prescribed in paragraphs a, b or f of this rule sound AN IDENTITY SIGNAL CONSISTING OF FOUR SHORT BLASTS.

Rule 37 – Distress signals

When a VESSEL is IN DISTRESS AND REQUIRES ASSISTANCE she shall use or exhibit the signals prescribed in Annex IV to these regulations:

a) a gun or other EXPLOSIVE SIGNAL fired at intervals of about a minute
b) a CONTINUOUS SOUNDING with any fog-signalling apparatus
c) ROCKETS OR SHELLS THROWING RED STARS fired one at a time at short intervals
d) a signal made by radiotelegraphy or by any other signalling method consisting of the group ···———··· [SOS] IN THE MORSE CODE
e) a signal sent by radiotelephony consisting of the SPOKEN WORD 'MAYDAY'
f) the INTERNATIONAL CODE SIGNAL of distress indicated by NC
g) a signal consisting of a SQUARE FLAG HAVING ABOVE OR BELOW IT A BALL or anything resembling a ball
h) FLAMES on the vessel [as from a burning tar barrel, oil barrel etc]
i) a rocket parachute flare or a hand FLARE SHOWING A RED LIGHT
j) a smoke signal giving off ORANGE-COLOURED SMOKE
k) slowly and repeatedly RAISING AND LOWERING ARMS outstretched to each side
l) the RADIOTELEGRAPH ALARM SIGNAL
m) the RADIOTELEPHONY ALARM SIGNAL
n) signals transmitted by EMERGENCY POSITION–INDICATING RADIO BEACONS

[Note that it is prohibited to use these signals except to indicate distress and the need for assistance.]

Annex I – Positioning and technical details of light and shapes
c) The masthead light of a power-driven vessel of 12 metres but less than 20 metres in length shall be placed at a height above the gunwale of not less than 2.5 metres.
d) A power-driven vessel of less than 12 metres in length may carry the uppermost light at a height of less than 2.5 metres above the gunwale. When however a masthead light is carried in addition to sidelights and a sternlight, then such masthead light shall be carried at least 1 metre higher than the sidelights.
h) The sidelights, if in a combined lantern and carried on a power-driven vessel of less than 20 metres in length shall be placed not less than 1 metre below the masthead light.

Annex II – Additional signals for fishing vessels

2 – Signals for trawlers
a) VESSELS WHEN ENGAGED IN TRAWLING (see plate 8), whether using demersal or pelagic gear, may exhibit:
  (i) WHEN SHOOTING THEIR NETS – TWO WHITE LIGHTS in a vertical line
  (ii) WHEN HAULING THEIR NETS – ONE WHITE LIGHT OVER ONE RED LIGHT in a vertical line
  (iii) WHEN THE NET HAS COME FAST UPON AN OBSTRUCTION – TWO RED LIGHTS in a vertical line
b) EACH VESSEL ENGAGED IN PAIR TRAWLING may exhibit:
  (i) by night, a SEARCHLIGHT directed forward and in the direction of the other vessel of the pair
  (ii) when shooting or hauling their nets or when their nets have come fast upon an obstruction, the lights prescribed in 2a above

3 – Signals for purse seiners
VESSELS ENGAGED IN FISHING WITH PURSE SEINE GEAR may exhibit TWO YELLOW LIGHTS in a vertical line. These lights shall FLASH ALTERNATELY EVERY SECOND with equal light and occultation duration. These lights may be exhibited only when the vessel is hampered by its fishing gear.

Safety equipment
There is no absolute safety at sea, any more than on land, so that any discussion of safety equipment and practice is a matter of personal judgment

Isolated danger mark

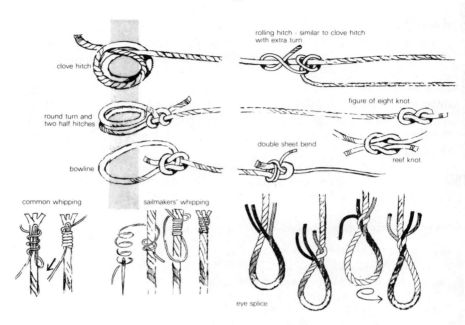

Knots and ropework. There are two basic types of synthetic rope, one conventionally twisted in three strands, the other plaited from a large number of strands. The first type is easy to splice, as illustrated; the second is soft and supple – making it ideal for sheets – and more complicated to splice. Another important distinction is between pre-stretched ropes (more suitable for halyards) and those that have all their original stretch in them. Nylon is more elastic than Terylene and, with this in mind, is used for anchor warps.

The knots you need for the Day Skipper/Watchleader qualification are pretty basic and probably familiar to most people. But if you are learning any of them from scratch try to remember the logic – why the rope leads from the left rather than the right, for instance, or why it goes under instead of over. Many yachtsmen nowadays simply seal the ends of synthetic ropes by burning them, but two of the traditional methods of whipping are included in the syllabus.

Perhaps the most common mistake in handling ropes aboard a modern yacht is to allow sheets to take a riding turn on the barrel of a winch – that is, allowing one turn to jam across another as one does quite deliberately in tying a rolling hitch. The result may be to jam sheet and winch solid. The solution is to ease the tension in some way – perhaps by attaching a strop forward of the winch – so that the turns can be slackened and freed.

and compromise. The standards listed below are largely based on the Department of Trade's recommendations for pleasure craft from 18 to 45 feet long (craft of more than 45 feet are subject to the Merchant Shipping Regulations) and on the RYA's own pamphlet *Safety Equipment for Cruising Yachts*. For examination purposes it will pay to err on the side of caution and whatever guidance your instructor offers.

One point on which there can be no argument is that everyone on board should have some sort of lifejacket. A proper lifejacket, as opposed to a buoyancy aid, is designed to turn an unconscious person on to his back and support his head well above water level. A lifejacket is defined by British Standard Specification BS 3595. The merit of some buoyancy aids, which, for example, double as an oilskin or a windproof waistcoat, is that you are more likely to be wearing them if you fall overboard accidentally.

The yacht should be carrying at least two lifebuoys (sometimes called liferings) for throwing to a man overboard (buoyant kapok-filled cushions also throw well) with a long floating line available if appropriate. At night, an automatic light attached to the lifebuoy, which comes on when it inverts in its floating position, could be a lifesaver. Even by day, keeping a continuous watch on the man overboard is one of the most vital aspects of the man overboard drill – and made easier if you can drop a tall dan buoy of the kind fishermen use to mark lobster pots.

At least enough safety harnesses to equip the watch on deck in bad weather or at night should be carried. Small children need them anyway and for sailing craft the Department of Trade recommends one for each person on board. The relevant standard is BS 4224, although most harnesses do not comply with it. When choosing attachment points, avoid the size of U bolt which will neatly prise open a spring hook when pulled across it. Attachment may be to jackstays rigged fore and aft on deck.

Yachts going offshore are recommended to carry a mixed pack of distress flares comprising four red parachute rockets (which can be seen from a great distance provided they are not fired into low cloud), four red hand flares, and two orange smoke signals (for high visibility by day). White flares are a valuable 'deterrent' to ships on a collision course at night which have apparently failed to see your navigation lights, your radar echo, or the powerful waterproof torch which should be carried for this and many other purposes.

Fire can be more dangerous at sea than on land, even though one is surrounded by water. Any yacht with either an engine or cooking equipment needs a fire extinguisher, and the average auxiliary cruising yacht

Papa

should carry at least two. As with flares, the price may seem high for something most yachtsmen never use in a lifetime's sailing, but when you want them, you want them badly. Large powerful motor yachts should have fixed fire extinguishing installations designed into their engine compartment. Other large yachts are recommended to carry two 3 lb (1.4 kg) dry powder extinguishers or the equivalent, and one of 5 lb (2.3 kg). For vessels of less than 30 feet, the two 3 lb extinguishers are considered adequate.

The alternatives to dry powder are carbon dioxide or foam. Extinguishers filled with BCF (bromo-chloro-difluoro-methane) or BTM (bromo-trifluoro-methane) may also be carried provided the crew understand that the fumes they produce are themselves dangerously toxic in a confined space. It is common sense to position the extinguishers at both ends of the boat so that a fire can be approached from either direction. Remember also that some fires can be smothered, ideally with a special fire blanket. Sea water is not the best thing to use inside a small boat, but a bucket on a lanyard is certainly worth having.

The main risks of fire and explosion come from the engine and the galley, and the most common combination of these two – a petrol engine and gas cooking – is potentially the most dangerous. With gas, the most important single precaution is to close the valve on the bottle when it is not needed. The gas is heavier than air, so if it does escape it will tend to sink into the bilges – which is why bottles are often stored in a separate locker that drains directly overboard. Petrol leaking from an engine or spilt while refuelling will also fill the bilges with dangerous fumes. A gas detector is one answer. Pumping out with a diaphragm pump is another.

Two pumps that are easy to dismantle and can be worked from secure positions, preferably either on deck or below, with all hatches closed, are in any case a basic piece of safety equipment. It may be a good idea to make one of them an electric pump, which keeps going when human beings tire. As a last resort, the bucket mentioned above may be invaluable.

The boat's first aid kit should include tablets for seasickness, dressings for burns and some kind of painkiller. But perhaps the most important item is a book of first aid instructions – including how to give mouth-to-mouth resuscitation or treat a case of hypothermia – because not knowing what to do for the best is sometimes the most frightening thing about an accident or injury. *Reed's Nautical Almanac* contains a section on first aid at sea, including a list of items recommended in a first aid kit (and some tips on delivering babies).

A radio receiver is not normally regarded as a piece of safety equipment, but at sea it certainly increases safety because it gives access to the BBC's gale warnings and weather forecasts.

Two anchors should be carried – a main bower, preferably with chain, and a smaller kedge which is easier to handle and lay out from a dinghy. The catenary of the heavy chain helps to maintain the required horizontal pull on the anchor and prevent the boat shearing around. If warp is used with the main anchor it should be made of nylon, and at least 3 fathoms of chain should in any case be attached to it at the anchor end.

The normal rule of thumb for anchoring with chain is to let out a length at least three times the depth of water, and with warp at least five times. The principles which distinguish the various types of anchor illustrated are their holding efficiency once they dig in (in soft ground the plough types hold much better, pound for pound, than the traditional fisherman or grapnel), the way they stow (some fold flat, for instance), and their ability to cope with different kinds of seabed. Each design has its own advocates, but it is safe to generalize that a fisherman anchor will cope better with kelp or seaweed, while a digging anchor is more suitable in sand and mud, or a sandy bottom strewn with rocks.

When choosing an anchoring berth, the first thing to check is the nature of the bottom. Then calculate the depth of water that will be left at low tide. Finally, imagine the berth in the worst conditions you are likely to encounter before you leave. Would you have room to sail the anchor out at low water in a freshening onshore breeze?

One piece of safety equipment that has become increasingly valuable as merchant ships get bigger, faster, and apparently more careless of their small sisters, is a radar reflector. The common type of reflector consists of three aluminium plates slotted together to form a complex shape known as an octahedral, hopefully presenting one of its 're-entrant trihedrals' – the same hollow shape formed at the corner of a room where the ceiling meets the walls – to bounce back the radar transmitter's beam and produce a blip on the ship's screen.

The reflector should be hoisted or fixed as high as possible – the minimum recommended height is 3 metres – in the position in which it would stand on a flat surface or catch water in its upper corner. The minimum effective size is about half a metre across. Perhaps the best all round installation is between a pair of twin backstays. But however well it is installed it cannot guarantee to send back a visible echo. It is simply a great deal better than nothing.

Much more efficient are the Firdell type reflectors, consisting of a

Yankee

collection of re-entrant trihedrals packed into a plastic cylinder so as to return a good echo in almost every direction. They hoist naturally in a correct position, and cause little windage or chafe.

Coping with bad weather

The most obvious kind of bad weather is a gale, but in a shipping lane like the Dover Strait, half choked with sandbanks and a ship passing on average every five minutes, fog can be just as much of a hazard – especially since sea fog can be combined with a fresh breeze that brings its own complications for small sailing craft. But at least the wind gives manoeuvrability, and removes the feeling of helplessness that comes with lying becalmed in poor visibility. If there are obviously ships about, it's a fine point of judgment as the wind drops off when to switch on an auxiliary engine, thereby exchanging the ability to hear danger approaching for the speed to get out of the way if it actually arrives.

Common sense fog precautions include plotting the most accurate possible position before it clamps down (this is when the methodical navigator scores), wearing lifejackets, having a dinghy ready to launch or cast off, and using a foghorn (although on a big ship's bridge it will not be heard in time). In some situations the safest course may be to sound your way into shallow water where large vessels cannot follow, and drop the anchor.

The key to surviving strong winds in relative comfort and safety is anticipation, starting with your yachtmaster's weather forecasting skill and a basic decision on whether to run for shelter or find some sea room to ride it out – a choice that even lifeboatmen have sometimes got wrong. In rough weather, especially if you cannot heave to, almost everything is much more difficult and tiring than usual, even just moving about or filling a kettle, and seasickness may make matters worse. The aim, therefore, is to reduce to a minimum the number of things that will have to be done during the blow by thinking ahead and making preparations – putting on oilskins before you get wet, stowing loose gear securely, sealing hatches, preparing some simple food, shortening sail early (unless you are racing, of course), looking up navigational data you may need, planning where you will bolt to if an unexpected gear failure forces you to run off downwind, and so on. If night is coming on, all this applies only more so.

The Coastguard

If you do ever have to fire distress flares, it will probably be the coastguard which organizes the rescue operation. The service was founded in 1822 to prevent smuggling. Nowadays its 600 regular officers and 800 auxiliaries guard the coast in a different sense. Each year they deal with more than 1000 incidents where craft are overdue or in distress, and their crucial assets in this work are a radio communications system and men with experience of using it.

There are six Maritime Rescue Co-ordination Centres round the British coast (on the Clyde, at Aberdeen, Yarmouth, Dover, Brixham and Swansea) plus a large number of sub-centres and stations, many of them manned 24 hours a day (if the flag is flying, there is someone there). Coastguard officers may not see the red flare themselves, or hear the Mayday, but if a yacht is reported in trouble they can ask for a lifeboat to be launched, call in a helicopter, alert ships in the vicinity, or send out one of their own launches. In the Dover Strait, they operate the Channel Navigation Information Service, using powerful surveillance radars to monitor ships – and yachts – using the IMO traffic separation scheme. We may sometimes forget **Rule 10** of the collision regulations, but they do not.

The coastguard also organizes a Yacht and Boat Safety Scheme to encourage closer contact between yachtsmen and their local rescue station, and invite them to supply it with details of their boat – name, colour, sail number, speed, radio equipment and so on – that might be useful in an emergency.

Passage planning

Getting out the charts and the tide tables to plan a passage can give a lot of pleasure in anticipation – better than the real thing in some cases – as well as saving time and trouble at sea. Time can be saved, for example, by planning to work your tides; by setting out so that you arrive at a navigational corner like the North Foreland as the tide turns in your favour; by arranging your coastal hops to avoid meeting the Portland race at full bore. If your destination is a river entrance with a tricky bar, you can save trouble by arriving on the flood rather than the ebb, and the same obviously goes for shallow swatchways through the sands. Going foreign, many navigators try to time their landfall for just before dawn, so as to make use of the lights to give an unmistakable fix, and then enter harbour in daylight.

As in preparing for a blow, anything that can be done in advance, before leaving harbour, will probably be easier than at sea – sorting out charts, looking up harbour entrance signals and noting them in the margin, plotting a couple of likely courses, and so on. If you are going foreign, you should

Snow

also give notice to HM Customs and Excise by completing Part I of Form C1328 and presenting it, either by hand or by post, at the nearest Customs office.

The French authorities have agreed to accept Parts II and III of this same form as an alternative to inspecting a yacht's certificate of registration, for British yachts making bona fide temporary (that is, not more than six months) visits before the end of 1983 – but only if Part I has been lodged with the British Customs. From 1 January 1984, the French say they will demand either a certificate of registration or the simplified equivalent the Department of Trade is introducing.

Returning from abroad, yachtsmen must fly the yellow Q flag on entering the UK's territorial waters, complete Parts II and III of C1328 and, on landing, inform the Customs of their arrival, in person or by telephone. If the vessel is not visited by a Customs officer within two hours, and provided she is not carrying prohibited goods or animals, and the crew have no more than their duty free allowances, clearance can be obtained by delivering Part II of the form, by hand or by post.

Well, that's it! We hope we have done our bit to help. The hard work is up to you and we wish you luck. And remember that when all's said and done, the only thing that finally makes seamen is sea time.